# The New York Times
## Guide to the Return of Halley's Comet

Alec J. Crockett
2115 W. Club Blvd.
Durham, N. C.,
June 1985

Father's Day from Dick

*By*
*Richard Flaste,*
*Holcomb Noble,*
*Walter Sullivan, and*
*John Noble Wilford*

𝕿𝖍𝖊 𝕹𝖊𝖜 𝖄𝖔𝖗𝖐 𝕿𝖎𝖒𝖊𝖘
*Guide to the Return of*

# HALLEY'S
# COMET

𝕿𝖎𝖒𝖊𝖘 BOOKS

Copyright © 1985 by Richard Flaste, Holcomb Noble, Walter Sullivan, and John Noble Wilford

All rights reserved under International and Pan-American Copyright Conventions. Published in the United States by Times Books, a division of Random House, Inc., New York, and simultaneously in Canada by Random House of Canada Limited, Toronto.

**Library of Congress Cataloging in Publication Data**

Main entry under title:

The New York Times guide to the return of Halley's comet.

Includes index.
1. Halley's comet.   2. Halley's comet—Amateurs' manuals.   I. Flaste, Richard.
QB723.H2N49   1985        523.6'4       84-40420
ISBN 0-8129-1148-2

Designed by Janis Capone

Manufactured in the United States of America

9 8 7 6 5 4 3 2

First Edition

**To Edmond**

Invaluable consultation and assistance were given by Dr. Kenneth Franklin, Astronomer at the American Museum-Hayden Planetarium, and Dr. Donald K. Yeomans of the Jet Propulsion Laboratory at the California Institute of Technology.

# Contents

# Halley's Comet:
# A Calendar

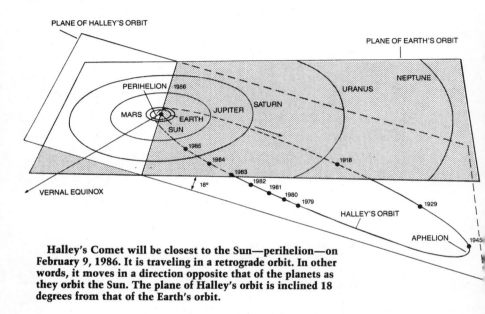

**Halley's Comet will be closest to the Sun—perihelion—on February 9, 1986. It is traveling in a retrograde orbit. In other words, it moves in a direction opposite that of the planets as they orbit the Sun. The plane of Halley's orbit is inclined 18 degrees from that of the Earth's orbit.**

**1948:** Halley's Comet, at aphelion or its most distant point from the Sun, beyond the orbit of Neptune, begins its return journey.

**1977:** Comet passes the orbit of Uranus.

**October 16, 1982:** Returning comet first sighted with the 200-inch telescope on Palomar Mountain, world's second largest such instrument. (The largest is in Zelenchukskaya, Soviet Union.)

**1983:** Comet passes the orbit of Saturn.

**December 1984:** Vega 1 and Vega 2 launched from the Soviet space center at Tyuratam.

**1985:** Comet passes the orbit of Jupiter.

**January 1985:** Japan launches its advance probe MS-T5.

**June 1985:** The two Vegas fly past Venus, whose gravity throws them toward a rendezvous with Halley.

**July 1985:** The European probe named Giotto is launched from French Guiana.

**August 1985:** The Japanese probe Planet A is launched from the Kagoshima Space Center.

**November 27, 1985:** Comet makes its closest approach to Earth while inbound, passing within 58 million miles. Designated a special Halley Watch Day.

**Early January 1986:** During evening twilight in midlatitudes of the United States the comet becomes visible with binoculars and small telescopes 35 degrees above the western horizon.

**January 20, 1986:** Comet visible with unaided eye 10 degrees above the western horizon during evening twilight. On subsequent days it comes so close to the Sun that it can no longer be seen.

**February 6–13, 1986:** Comet circles the Sun; is closest to Sun on February 9.

**February 24, 1986:** Comet reappears in the morning sky a few degrees above the eastern horizon at dawn twilight.

**March 6, 1986:** The Soviet spacecraft Vega 1 to pass within 6,000 miles of the comet's nucleus. In central United States latitudes the comet, perhaps with a short tail, will be 5 degrees above the eastern horizon during dawn twilight.

**March 9, 1986:** Vega 2 passes within 2,000 miles of the comet.

**Early March 1986:** Japan's two probes make their closest approach to the comet.

**March 13–14, 1986:** Giotto, the European probe, passes 300 miles on Sun-facing side of the comet.

**March 26, 1986:** Comet in dawn sky 10 degrees above the southeastern horizon; tail may reach up to 20 degrees or more.

**April 10, 1986:** Close to maximum apparent brightness, 10 degrees above the southern horizon at the start of dawn twilight.

**April 11, 1986:** Comet, outbound, closest to Earth for this apparition, passing within 39 million miles.

**April 12, 1986:** Comet is in "solar conjunction," close to the Earth-Sun line. It is visible before dawn in the southwest and after sunset in the southeast, but very low in the sky.

**April 17, 1986:** In the southeast 7 degrees above the horizon after sunset.

**End of April 1986:** Visible in the south only with optical aids 32 degrees above the southern horizon after sunset.

**March 1987:** Comet passes orbit of Jupiter, outbound.

**1990 or later:** Comet possibly still visible with the Space Telescope as it nears outer limits of its orbit beyond Neptune.

# The New York Times
## Guide to the Return of Halley's Comet

# Earthward Bound

**Waiting for the Comet** Halley's Comet is coming in from the cold again, a homely lump of dust and gas speeding toward Earth and beyond, for its loop around the Sun.

A lonely voyager, journeying through the Solar System in an orbit all its own, Halley's Comet will grow brighter over time, and its image will expand as if it were some kind of cosmic peacock finally getting its chance to show off. This splendid transformation will be accomplished not merely by passively reflected light of the sort that gives the Moon its dramatic presence. It will be much more. For the comet will literally give of itself, shedding tiny pieces of its core as it approaches the Sun, and these agitated bits will phosphor and glow so that the comet becomes a sparkler in the heavens. As it approaches, the excitement is palpable on Earth among the only organisms in all the Solar System with the wit to name the comet and to try to come to grips with it, to wonder about it, to try to know it.

As the voyager heads in from the void and the anticipation of the people on Earth heightens, there is a prayerful wish among those who know a thing or two about astronomical drama and cosmic disap-

1

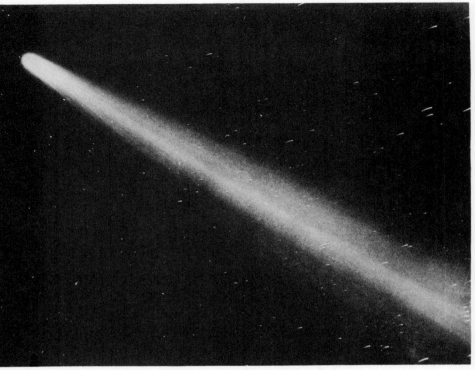

Halley's comet in 1910. *(Jet Propulsion Laboratory)*

pointment: Let this one go right. Let it be a spectacle
for mankind to see and a vein of knowledge for scientists to mine. And if it cannot be so great a spectacle in the light-polluted cities, then let it be fine in
the darkened countryside. And if it is less than mar-
velous in the Northern Hemisphere, then let it be
wonderful in the Southern. But please, whatever
happens, don't let it be another Kohoutek.

Kohoutek—one hesitates to speak its name—was,
of course, a fiasco. At least so it seemed at the time.
Painful though it may be to recall the story, it is perhaps useful to do so here at the outset, as a kind of
cautionary tale. Kohoutek was supposed to be fan-
tastic—"awesome" was a common way of describ-

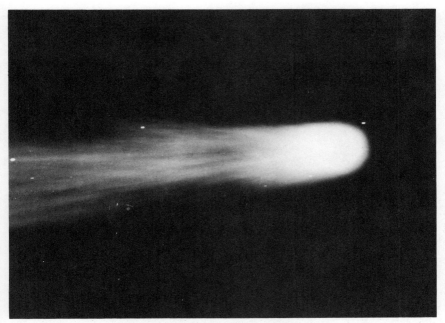

**The head of Halley's Comet in 1910.**

ing how it would seem to the admiring eyes of man. It was the fall of 1973, and most astronomers, *The New York Times* reported, believed the comet "will produce an awesome spectacle for all humanity, and they are excited about the opportunity they believe it offers, at long last, to learn what comets really are." It was supposed to be the most brilliant comet of the century—perhaps, as one writer put it, "the biggest, brightest, most spectacular astral display that living man has ever seen"—surpassing even Halley's 1910 apparition (a lovely cometspeak word that refers to the seeing of the comet).

But typical of this forlorn event was the experience of the passengers on the *Queen Elizabeth 2*, somewhere off the coast of Delaware. They had all spent $295 for a voyage whose star would be a comet, and aboard ship in the supporting cast was

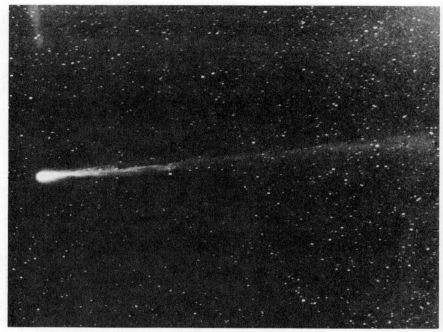

Comet Kohoutek coursed by Earth in December of 1973,
amid great excitement. But, although it was useful to
scientists, it proved to be a disappointing sight. Here it is
seen with the aid of a telescope at the Joint Observatory for
Cometary Research, South Baldy Mountain, New Mexico.
(NASA)

none other than the Czech astronomer Dr. Lubos
Kohoutek, the man who had discovered the thing.
Well, the cloud cover was rather thick, as luck
would have it, so the comet was in no way visible.
Nor, for much of the trip, was Dr. Kohoutek, who
was suffering from jet lag and stayed in his state-
room.

Even when it was visible, Comet Kohoutek was
no great shakes. Scientists, then as now, know too
little to estimate brightness precisely. With Kohoutek, they were far off. In Boston, one resident peered
into the heavens with his binoculars, saw no more

than a fuzzy blur, and decided right then that he'd already had enough of the 1970s. "Watergate," he muttered, "the energy crisis—and now the comet." One headline writer called it a "Cosmic Flopperoo." And yet what had the comet done to deserve such universal derision?

It had let us down. But the truth is that it did not let *all* of us down. For scientists, this comet would ultimately yield up important information (although it would not answer anything like all the pressing questions scientists still have about the makeup of these mysterious travelers). And, after all, Earth was a mere way station for Kohoutek on a centuries-long journey that would take in the Sun, Pluto, and more. Let us down. So what.

The disappointment speaks more to the nature of man than it does to the nature of comets. One part of man is intellectual, wanting to satisfy its curiosity about these small, sparkling celestial bodies. What are they really made of? (There are good hypotheses, of course, but they are only hypotheses.) And is it true, as some have postulated, that comets carry with them the most basic building material that began life on Earth? Was it they that seeded the waters and gave rise to algae, fish, chimpanzees, and man?

But beyond the intellectual, scientific questioning, there is some forceful spiritual need these comets address. It is almost an unquenchable need, evidently. Even the enormous disappointment brought by Kohoutek seems to have done nothing to lessen the spiritual attraction of comets. Each time one comes by, it brings with it again the same almost childish thrill that has its roots somewhere in man's primal past. When the comet named IRAS-Araki-Alcock coursed past Earth in 1983, the excitement was there anew. People would climb to their rooftops once more. This one was not big, but it would be close—closer than any other comet in recorded history, just 2.9 million miles from Earth.

On May 11, 1983, Comet IRAS-Araki-Alcock passed just three million miles from Earth. The photo was taken at the Oak Ridge Observatory. *(Dennis Milon)*

Astronomers scrambled to make the most of it, as in great numbers they called the Smithsonian Astrophysical Observatory in Cambridge, Massachusetts, a clearinghouse of cometary information, for precise information on the comet's trajectory. For the astronomer Brian Marsden, a comet specialist, it was the most hectic time he could remember in his entire career. But, shades of Kohoutek, the IRAS wasn't much to see either, just a fuzzy blob in the night sky. It served at least one great purpose, however. It was a valuable impromptu rehearsal for the arrival of the most valued comet of all, Comet Halley.

The first recorded flyby of this comet was in 467 B.C. Unnamed, until its orbit of about seventy-six years was calculated by Newton's friend Edmond Halley in 1695, the spectacular voyager was known simply and respectfully as The Comet. The mere naming of it after Halley, however, did little to assuage man's fear and reverence for The Comet. The

Norman invasion of England in 1066 was influenced by Comet Halley, or so thinkers on the world scene thought at the time. Medieval pestilence, too, was associated with the coming of this orb of gas and dust.

In 1910, despite much sophistication, there was nevertheless a startling amount of lunacy attached to this astral event. People were persuaded that when Earth passed through the tail of the comet, a gas they called cyanogen would snuff out life. As it happened, the only way the tail of the comet impaired anyone's breathing was through the mortal grip of anxiety. (It may have been crazy to fear the cyanogen gas, but anxiety about cometary destruction—in light of some modern thinking that links cometary collisions with Earth to periodic extinctions of some life forms here—does not seem to be entirely misplaced.)

Now it is coming again, bearing with it a burden of uncertainty, as usual. Especially, there is that question of how visible it will be. There is virtually no doubt that the comet will be well seen in the Southern Hemisphere. The difficult question is this: How exciting will it be in the northern latitudes? As the eighties wore on, astronomers seemed painfully aware of the Kohoutek experience and their predictions were laced with caution more than promise. Even the most cautious among them, however, believed the comet would be visible in the north if one used an appropriate pair of binoculars—the so-called night glasses that were familiar in World War II—and found a dark place to watch the sky. It was believed firmly that the comet would have a discernible tail, which would begin to form in March of 1985 (although only the most accomplished observers would see it then). A year before the tail began to form, it was clear that comet buffs on Earth were already making plans to take their vacations in the winter and spring of 1985–86 as far south as they

could arrange to be for Halley's encounter with
Earth. Florida would be better than New York and
Barbados better than Florida. Australia would be just
splendid.

Whatever this return of Comet Halley might
mean to the casual observer, there was no doubt at
all that it would be the impetus for one of the greatest scientific spectaculars ever staged by the nations
of the world. The comet had once—in science's
darker ages when people believed angry, vengeful
forces controlled the heavens—played a momentous
scientific role. By demonstrating its predictability it
had proved theories born of the genius of Copernicus, Galileo, Tycho Brahe, Kepler, Newton, and of
course the lesser known astronomer, Edmond Halley. Now, it was about to play a magnificent role
again.

A new era of astronomy was clearly upon us. Scientists were no longer limited to observing the universe and exploring it with the limited powers of
their eyes alone. They now had instruments that
could record gamma rays, X rays, and infrared radiation from objects in space. Exotic celestial objects
such as quasars, pulsars, and supernovas emit most
of their radiation in these remote invisible areas of
the electromagnetic spectrum. And where once observatories were bound to the Earth, perched on high
mountains as they strained toward space, now those
observatories could be thrust above the atmosphere
into space itself. Thus atmospheric interference was
rapidly becoming a barrier of the past. There was the
sense in the mideighties that, as each new observatory was sent into orbit, it would carry with it the
power to see fiery elements of the universe never
before seen—stars being born, perhaps, or stars that
had never been known before. Evidence of black
holes might be seen. The universe was about to lose
a great many of its secrets. "There's no question,"

said one prominent astronomer, "that astronomers will look back on this period as a golden age."

Into that aura of scientific optimism plunged Comet Halley, a perfect object to test out the new age of astronomy. As it raced toward Earth, where all these new inventions and new capabilities were poised to explore the cosmos, it was still true that very little was known about comets. As to the most fundamental question of all—what are they?—the strongest assumption held that a comet was a "dirty snowball," mostly an ice ball of water and frozen carbon dioxide, ammonia, and other gases. In that ice ball, according to prevailing theory, were grains of dust made of carbon and other elements. But which ones no one could say for sure. As any comet hurtles toward Earth, it is obscured by a coma, the glowing envelope that surrounds the nucleus as the comet becomes increasingly agitated on its flight toward the warmth of the Sun. Thus, no one even knows exactly how big the hidden nucleus is. This time around there should be some answers.

And more.

To find some answers, the scientific powers of the world—from the laboratories of Europe to the command centers in the Soviet Union to the observatories in the United States and to the fledgling space program of Japan—will be mounting an awe-inspiring, orchestrated effort that will track the comet as it has never been tracked before and then chase it through space. Their observatories on land and in space will examine the comet in broad sweep and in minute detail. One spacecraft, the Giotto sent aloft by the Europeans, will pass so close to Comet Halley on the night of March 13–14 in 1986 that there is every expectation it will be destroyed by a blast of cometary dust. But before it is obliterated, this craft, like the others, should be able to send back to Earth streams of data on the tangible realities of the comet. Giotto will be among the instruments to photograph the comet's nucleus to determine its size, mass, and rotational characteristics. Among its capabilities, Giotto can photograph the comet. The photography will begin only ten minutes before the closest encounter and cease with the craft's destruction.

Radio astronomy will help confirm whether or not water is a major component of comets and identify other molecules. Spectroscopy will dissect the light from the comet and identify chemicals through their unique spectral signatures. Infrared readings, which led to the identification of silicate dusts in Comet Kohoutek will be used here, too. The close analysis of Halley's every movement should finally tell astronomers whether the course of the comet is determined in some significant way by bursts of its own gases in addition to the gravitational pull that keeps it in orbit around the Sun.

To a large extent, how much we learn about this comet depends on how well we've learned to ask questions. And it will depend on how sure-handed we are with the new technology. It is a technology, after all, that despite limitless promise often founders on the little mistakes. The wondrous Solar Max satellite was sent aloft to study the Sun and promptly went into cardiac arrest when a fuse blew at the heart of its workings; it had to be rescued and repaired by the United States space shuttle, a piece of machinery that has also given us a thrill or two when surprising little failures threatened grand endeavors.

Even if through some colossal blunder we manage to learn very little about the comet, we may learn a great deal about international cooperation. For that, the comet couldn't be coming by at a better time. Scientifically and politically, the mideighties have been a period of frigid relations between East and West. The exploration of space is one shining exception. And as for the comet's gift to individuals on Earth, whatever else happens, each of us stands a good chance of becoming more intimate with the heavens as we peer at our star charts and come to know the sky.

Three centuries ago John Bunyan wrote in Part II of *Pilgrim's Progress* about a man who "could look no way but downwards, with a muck-rake in his hand. There stood also one over his head, with a celestial crown in his hand, and proffered him that crown for his muck-rake; but the man did neither look up, nor regard, but raked to himself the straws, the small sticks, and dust of the floor."

This time many of us will look up, to be sure, and it just may be that we are standing, poised for the Enlightenment thrust toward us by Edmond Halley but slow in getting here.

# Halley
# and
# Friends

At half past six in the morning of November 22, 1682, Edmond Halley got his first glimpse of the comet that would bear his name and assure his enduring fame. He was looking through a telescope at his home in Islington, near London. He was not the first to see the comet that year; a German astronomer, Georg Samuel Dorffel, had sighted it three months earlier and alerted his colleagues throughout Europe. He was not the only one to plot its course with care; the Rev. John Flamsteed, the Astronomer Royal, was making even more detailed observations at Greenwich. Nor was this the most spectacular comet ever to hold mankind in thrall; dazzling though it was, many other comets through the ages, and as recently as 1680, had been as bright or brighter and had provoked more fear and inspired as much wonder among all those who looked up into the heavens. What Halley did, however, made the comet he studied in November 1682 the most important of all comets.

*The People, the Theories, the Facts*

The comet could not have come at a better time or have had a better witness than Halley, who embodied the intellectual and scientific vitality of the late

seventeenth century in England. It was the time of
Isaac Newton, whose revolutionary insights into the
nature of gravity would soon be published with the
encouragement and assistance of Halley. It was the
time of Robert Boyle, the father of modern chemistry, whose research upset Aristotle's venerable notion that all matter falls into the four categories of
earth, air, fire, and water. It was the time of John
Milton's poetry, John Locke's philosophy, Henry
Purcell's music, and Christopher Wren's churches.
Samuel Pepys was writing his diaries, and the London of that day afforded ample material for his obser-
vant eye and ranging mind.

There was good reason for Londoners to believe
that they were entering a golden age. In any event,
they were succeeding in putting behind them a recent past of tumult and tribulation. After an inter-
regnum of civil war, when Oliver Cromwell and the
Dissenters held sway, the monarchy was restored in
1660 under Charles II. The Restoration brought
order and royal patronage of the arts and sciences.
The Royal Society was established in 1662 under a
royal charter and began encouraging scientific in-
quiry by methods freer than ever from the constraints of myth, dogma, and superstition. Charles
also created in 1675 the Royal Observatory at Greenwich, where astronomers could contemplate the
mysteries of the cosmos and address such practical
matters as accurate timekeeping and navigation.
London itself had recovered handsomely from the
plague years and the Great Fire of 1666, which had
raged for five days through the heart of the city. By
the time of the 1682 comet, the city had rebounded
in number and fortune. The lot of the poor remained
wretched, and religious nonconformists were often
treated shabbily, but an outlook of expansive optimism was the rule. The salons and coffeehouses
were alive with talk of politics, commerce, faraway
places, and scientific ideas. There was, all in all, a

feeling that London was the center of the modern world and a fit place from which to observe and perhaps explain the universe.

Edmond Halley was very much at home in this world. He was born there, at his family's country house in Haggerston, outside London, on November 8, 1656—when "his" comet was twenty-six years away from its rendezvous with the Sun. His grandfather, Humphrey Halley, was a haberdasher and vintner. His father, Edmond Halley, Sr., was a soap maker and property owner. Not a family of high estate, perhaps, but one of comfortable means. The father recognized early the "promising genius" of young Edmond and saw to it that he was provided with books and the "curious apparatus" for observing the planets and stars. At St. Paul's School, Edmond became interested in the "new philosophy" of science, though it was the oldest science of astronomy that most appealed to him. Later, Halley would write that "from my tenderest youth I gave myself over to the consideration of Astronomy." It gave him, he said, "so much great pleasure as is impossible to explain to anyone who has not experienced it."

Astronomy was in the midst of a revolution that had begun more than a century earlier and had been fought mostly on the Continent. In 1543, the Polish scholar, Nicolas Copernicus, had exposed the notion of an Earth-centered universe as nothing more than a human conceit. The Sun did not move around a fixed Earth; the Earth moved around the Sun. Three of the greatest astronomers then came along with evidence supporting Copernicus, directly or indirectly. Tycho Brahe, the Danish astronomer, made meticulous observations of the other planets' movements, and Johannes Kepler, the German who inherited Tycho's notes and tables, determined that the orbit of a planet was not circular, as had been assumed, but was an ellipse with the Sun at one focus.

(Above) Johannes Kepler, making a point before Holy Roman Emperor Rudolf II, determined that the orbit of a planet was not circular but elliptical. *(New York Public Library)*

(Right) Tycho Brahe. *(New York Public Library)*

**Galileo Galilei was tried by the tribunal of the Roman Catholic Church for his assertion that Earth must be moving around the Sun; he recanted.**

This became Kepler's first law of planetary motion. And it could not have been more pleasing to mathematicians, because an ellipse, a sort of squashed circle, is one of the simplest closed curves on a plane, and thus relatively easy to calculate from periodic observations of a planet's movement in the sky. Meanwhile, Galileo Galilei in 1609 had peered through the first telescope at Jupiter and seen for the first time the four large satellites orbiting the giant planet. This was a revelation confirming Copernican theory. The moons of Jupiter were moving about this large body much as the planets of the Solar System, Earth included, must be moving about the Sun. Galileo's conclusion could not have been less pleasing to the Roman Catholic Church, which gave Galileo a choice of recanting or facing torture. One heretic holding similar views, Giordano Bruno, had

already been burned at the stake in Rome in 1600. So
Galileo recanted, but never changed his mind. Years
later, in 1665, Newton sat under the legendary apple
tree and, contemplating the falling apple, began to
ponder the forces that accounted for what Copernicus had theorized and Tycho, Kepler, and Galileo
had seen.

Halley could hardly wait to join the revolution. In
1673, at the age of seventeen, he enrolled at Queen's
College, Oxford, where he excelled in classics and
mathematics. For the rest of his life he delighted in
writing poetry in Latin. The accomplishment that
linked his name to the 1682 comet was essentially a
mathematical tour de force. But at the outset of his
university career, Halley proved himself to be a
gifted observational astronomer as well, and he
seemed to know it. He did not lack for self-con-
fidence. While at Oxford, he initiated a correspondence with Flamsteed, England's preeminent
astronomer, sharing with him his own telescopic observations. In his first letter to Flamsteed, the eigh-
teen-year-old Halley reported observations showing
that some published tables of planetary positions for
Jupiter and Saturn were in error. This led to his first
published scientific report. Flamsteed acknowledged
Halley to be "an ingenious youth well versed in calculations and almost all parts of mathematics, tho'
yet scarce 19 years of age."

Not waiting to graduate from Oxford, Halley at
the age of twenty embarked on an expedition to the
island of St. Helena. He was impatient to establish
his reputation as a professional astronomer. St.
Helena, which would later become famous as Napo-
leon's refuge in exile, lay below the Equator in the
Atlantic off Africa. There Halley went, through the
good offices of Charles II and the East India Company, which controlled the island, and with some
money from his father, to observe and chart the stars
in the southern sky. The northern skies had already

been well charted, by Flamsteed in particular, but
not the southern skies. Undaunted by a run of bad
weather, Halley persevered. By the time he returned
to London in 1678, he was prepared to compile an
authoritative catalog of 341 southern stars. The catalog's publication, the first such work to include
telescopically determined locations of southern
stars, brought him a master's degree from Oxford
and election to the Royal Society. He thus joined the
elite of British science in 1680 at the age of twenty-
three. The young man in a hurry had arrived.

Next, Halley decided to do what young English
gentlemen often did—to make a leisurely grand tour
of the Continent, to savor Paris before he settled
down, and to roam through Italy. And so he did,
leaving London in December 1680. Of the other en-
chantments he may have found Halley left no record; he kept no diary at any time in his life and left
few letters. His most memorable experience in
Paris, it would seem from the evidence at hand, was
with a glittering comet.

In November before he set forth, Halley had become fascinated with a comet that appeared, visible
to the naked eye, in the skies over London. The
comet, an exceptionally bright one, became the talk
of the town, for comets then were still very much
enigmas wrapped in myth and ignorance. No one
knew what they were, where they came from, or
what courses they followed getting from wherever
they originated to wherever they went. But there it
was in the sky for a few nights, and then it disappeared. On the way to Paris, Halley saw the
comet again and grew even more excited. (As is now
known, but was not generally recognized then, the
comet had been heading toward the Sun when it was
visible in November, had disappeared behind the
Sun, and was now in mid-December back in view as
it emerged from the other side of the Sun.) Halley
made haste to the Paris Observatory, which had

been established by the reigning Louis XIV. It was directed by Jean Dominique Cassini, the Italian-born scientist who founded a four-generation dynasty of Cassinis that dominated French astronomy for over a century and produced the first topographic map of an entire country. Cassini let the young Englishman examine the comet at the observatory and shared his records on the comet's movements.

Using these data, Halley made his first attempt to plot a comet's course through the heavens, the kind of calculations that would one day bring him a certain immortality. But this time, with the comet of 1680, he made a hash of it. The fault lay not in Halley's mathematics, but in the conventional scientific wisdom about comets. It was wrong. And so, in following it, was Halley.

Halley need not have felt embarrassed by his failure. No one else knew quite what to make of comets and their peculiar ways. Perhaps no one ever would, or so it seemed. In the first issue of the Royal Society's *Philosophical Transactions*, published in 1665, a certain M. Auzout, described as "a French gentleman of no ordinary Merit and Learning," wrote of his attempt to predict the movements of the comet of 1664. The author proudly referred to his project as "a design which never yet was undertaken by any Astronomer, all the World having been hitherto persuaded that the motions of Comets were so irregular, that they could not be reduced to any Laws." Auzout's results were not likely to persuade the world otherwise. He had no idea at all of the curve the comet followed in its course. In a second report the following year, he returned to the problem, this time concerning the course of a comet that appeared in 1665, and was no more successful. How could he have been? So little was known about the movements of comets, or of the Earth for that matter. A remark Auzout made, concerning the "Great Question whether the Earth moves or not," was revealing of the state of astronomical knowledge.

This much, and little more, was known about comets in the time Halley first essayed to plot their course: They were not, as Aristotle had affirmed, atmospheric phenomena. Aristotle had divided the universe into two distinct sectors. There were the regions below the Moon, full of change and streaking comets that became known as sublunary exhalations. Comets were supposed to be phenomena of the upper air, in a class with the northern lights. And then, according to Aristotle, there were the regions beyond the Moon, where nothing ever changed. Tycho, in the century before Halley, had demolished both of these concepts. He had seen a "new" star suddenly appear in the sky and, after months of careful measurements, satisfied himself that change did occur out beyond the Moon, Aristotle notwithstanding. Tycho addressed Aristotle's sublunary concept in making measurements of the great comet of 1577. He compared the apparent positions of the comet as seen from his observatory on an island between Denmark and Sweden with simultaneous sightings made hundreds of miles away in other parts of Europe. The position of the Moon was different at the widely separated viewing sites. But there was no perceptible difference in the position of the comet. Therefore, Tycho concluded, the comet had to be far beyond the Moon.

There was nothing but confusion on other aspects of comets. Were they true members of the Solar System? Did they orbit the Sun or were they plunging in on a straight line from outer space? Definitive answers were not easy to come by. A comet is only visible for a short period of time—a matter of days or a few weeks, in the age before telescopes and for two or three centuries afterward. In this brief period of visibility, astronomers at best could observe the comet for only a short section of its path among the background of stars. It was impossible to conclude from this whether the comet was traveling a straight line (the evidence from a short section of its path tended to suggest this) or a curved path of some kind. The possibilities of a curving course were several: a circle, an ellipse, a parabola, or the more open curve known as a hyperbola.

Tycho, though he rejected the idea of Copernicus that the Earth moved, was Copernican in his belief that the planets and the comet of 1577 were orbiting the Sun. Kepler, though he established the laws by which objects orbit the Sun in ellipses, did not believe that comets obeyed his laws of planetary motion. Comets, he said, traveled roughly in a straight line. He conceded that two comets he studied in the early seventeenth century did not appear to follow a straight-line course. But that, according to Kepler, was an illusion caused by the Earth's own movement.

Accepting this kind of Keplerian thinking, as they generally did, scientists of that day assumed that comets wandered through space until they happened to come close to the Sun. They might fall into the Sun and be destroyed. Or, missing the Sun, they might swing around it and return to outer space. It was very unlikely, many scientists believed, that any particular comet would ever return to the Solar System a second time. This was part of conventional wisdom when Halley became intrigued with comets.

Indeed, one of the best astronomers of the time, Johannes Hevelius of Danzig, had reaffirmed the straight-line theory in a somewhat modified form. In a book published in 1668, Hevelius explained that comets were disk-shaped bodies flung out of planets. Little wonder, then, that Halley approached his calculations of the 1680 comet on the assumption that he was seeing an object traveling a roughly straight-line course. There were even those who doubted that the comet seen in November and the one seen

in December were one and the same object. When
Flamsteed wrote to Newton suggesting the two appearances were of the same comet, Newton was po-
litely incredulous.

Halley never forgot the frustrating experience
of trying to calculate the path of the 1680 comet
and getting nowhere because he could not make the
data he had square with the accepted concept of a
straight-line course. On his return to London, after
more than a year on the Continent, he married Mary
Tooke and assumed an increasingly active role in
the Royal Society. He was a tall, lean, and quite sociable young man. He took an interest in all realms
of science, not just astronomy and mathematics, and
made fast friendships with many of his scientific el-
ders. His friendship with Robert Hooke, the in-
ventor and microscopist who was a founding
member of the Royal Society, apparently drove a
permanent wedge between Halley and his former
mentor, Flamsteed. Rivalry, jealousy, and pettiness
are no more alien to science than to any other human endeavor. Flamsteed, a dour, unhappy man,
could not abide Hooke or Newton and, therefore,
would have little more to do with Halley as he gravi-
tated into the Hooke-Newton orbit.

This happened as Halley, remembering the 1680
comet, began to ponder the larger problem of planetary motions. This was on his mind as he studied the
comet of 1682, "his" comet, from his home observatory at Islington. This was a problem also very
much on the minds of several of Halley's associates
in the Royal Society. There must be some kind of
gravitational force accounting for the motions of the
planets and moons and other bodies of the Solar System. But what exactly were the laws governing this
force, and how could they be proved?

In January 1684, Halley met with Hooke and
Christopher Wren, the architect, at a London coffeehouse, as was their habit, and fell into a long, earnest

Edmond Halley. *(The Royal Society)*

discussion of the problem. It was a fateful meeting, for it prompted Halley to pay the visit to Newton that led him to recognize the import of what Newton had wrought in his mind but was seemingly too shy and fearful to publish. And Halley's subsequent involvement with Newton, as his goad and editor and benefactor, led in time to Halley's discovery of the periodic character of comets and his correct prediction of when the 1682 comet would return again to the inner Solar System. This discovery—that the same comet might and actually did return again and again—followed as a natural consequence of Newton's great discovery of the Law of Gravitation. It was, indeed, the first direct confirmation of Newton's theories.

This chain of momentous events was set in motion when, at their coffeehouse meeting, Halley, Hooke, and Wren talked about a possible law of gravity that would explain the motions of all bodies in the Solar System. Halley proposed that the force of attraction must vary inversely with the square of the distance between a planet and the Sun. This, he noted, fitted well with Kepler's third law that connected the time a planet took to orbit and its distance from the Sun. But Halley confessed that, try as he might, he could think of no way to prove this idea. The mathematics were beyond him. Wren said that he had tried his hand at the problem and been equally unsuccessful. Hooke agreed with Halley's proposal and hinted that he just might have arrived at the mathematical proof based on the inverse square law. Now Wren knew of Hooke's propensity to boast a little too much. Sometimes his boasts were justified, but often they were not. So Wren, thinking to bring out the truth, offered a valuable book as the prize to the one who should come up with the solution first. Halley had no more luck, and Hooke seems to have procrastinated.

Halley then decided to consult Newton at Cam-

A portrait of Sir Isaac Newton by Sir Godfrey Kneller.
*(National Portrait Gallery)*

bridge. As H. H. Turner, a professor of astronomy at Oxford in the early twentieth century, remarked, "When did ever an Oxford man take a journey to Cambridge of such vital importance to the world!" It was in August of 1684.

Halley got to the point of his visit when he asked Newton, What would be the curve described by the planets on the supposition that gravity diminished as the square of the distance? Without hesitation, Newton replied that the curve would be an ellipse. How did he know that? "I have calculated it," replied Newton. Halley was eager to see these calcu-

lations. Newton searched through his papers but
could not find the notes containing his theorems
and proofs. He had done the work a few years back,
stimulated by some correspondence with Hooke,
and then laid the notes aside. He had not sent the
calculations to Hooke out of a fear, not entirely misplaced, that Hooke might seize some of the credit for
himself. Before Halley left, he extracted from Newton a promise to reproduce the calculations and send
the results to Halley.

This Newton did before the year was out. According to Colin A. Ronan, in his 1967 book *Astronomers Royal*, it is fortunate that Newton sent the
material to Halley and not to Wren or Hooke. "If it
had gone to Wren," Ronan wrote, "it might have received the prize but no more, if to Hooke there
would doubtless have been arguments about this
point or that; but Halley, a very good mathematician, not only found that Wren's problem had been
solved—he had the perception to see that here was
something far more significant. Newton had produced the concept of universal gravitation—falling
bodies on Earth with falling bodies in space."

Historians of science suspect that but for Halley
the world might not have learned from Newton the
laws of gravitation explaining the motions of the
Moon, the planets, and the comets as well. These
insights would undoubtedly have occurred to someone else sometime later. But they had already been
divined by Newton, and Halley realized it and, with
tact and persistence, guided Newton to the publication in 1687 of his great work *Philosophiae Natu-
ralis Principia Mathematica*, or the *Mathematical
Principles of Natural Philosophy*. Newton acknowledged his debt to Halley, writing in the book's pref-
ace that the "most acute and universally learned"
Halley corrected errors and prepared the geometrical
figures; it was, Newton said, "through his solicita-
tions that it came to be published." Acting for the

Royal Society, Halley coaxed the manuscript (written in Latin) out of Newton, edited it, and supervised and financed its printing. This was a little odd: Newton could have afforded to pay for the printing himself and Halley, though once rather wealthy, could not really afford it. It was surely one of the more generous examples of cooperation and selfless sponsorship in the annals of science.

In the *Principia*, Newton enunciated the way multiple forces operate together, the impact of one body on another, and the law of universal gravitation. He went on to use these laws of motion to explain the orbits of the satellites around Jupiter that Galileo had discovered and the orbits of the planets around the Sun, taking into account Kepler's laws. He showed how Kepler's laws of planetary motions are a natural consequence of the law of universal gravitation. In particular, Newton was apparently the first to conclude that Kepler's third law connecting the periods of the planets with their distances from the Sun resulted from an attractive force in the Sun varying inversely as the square of the distance. Then, spurred by Hooke's correspondence, Newton proved that under such a force a body would describe an ellipse with the Sun as its focus. (As Newton was completing the manuscript, Hooke created a furor at a Royal Society meeting with his claims that, in effect, he had provided Newton with all the key insights he was about to publish as his own. Halley had to mediate the dispute and soothe Newton's temper, lest he abandon the project altogether.) As a third step, Newton proposed and proved that a sphere would attract as though all its mass were concentrated at its center. Without this understanding, the application of the law of gravitation to the movements of the heavenly bodies would have been a mere approximation.

Halley naturally thought about comets when he contemplated the meaning of Newton's message. As

Halley said in his dedicatory ode to Newton, written
in Latin and included in the *Principia:*

> . . . *Now we know*
> *The sharply veering ways of comets, once*
> *A source of dread, nor longer do we quail*
> *Beneath appearances of bearded stars.*

Newton had spoken and clarified matters. Comets
did not travel in straight lines. They followed
"sharply veering" curves, probably parabolas or very
elongated ellipses. Newton suggested that comets
were "planets of a sort, revolving in orbits that return into themselves with a continual motion."

Still, Halley did not pursue the matter of cometary
courses with much diligence for another ten years or
so. He had many other things on his mind, for he
was a scientist of many parts: meteorology and biol-
ogy, oceanography and the physics of magnetism,
cartography and demography. This was long before
the fragmentation of science into narrow speciali-
zation; even so, few of his contemporaries could
match Halley in the breadth of his scientific interests.

Halley was an innovative cartographer. In 1686,
he drew what is considered the first meteorological
chart, which illustrated the directions of prevailing
winds over the oceans. Through such maps, Halley
observed, certain phenomena "may be better under-
stood, than by any verbal description whatsoever."
This was the beginning of what is known as the-
matic maps, maps that illustrate the geographic distribution of information about climate, vegetation,
population, wealth, or just about any physical or ab-
stract fact. Several years later, beginning in 1698,
Halley commanded a small warship, *Paramour*,
on voyages into the Atlantic where he plotted the
variations of the Earth's magnetism. On the map he
produced to illustrate these variations, Halley intro-

duced another of his cartographic innovations, the isolines. These are lines on a map connecting points of equal value, the most familiar of which today are the contour lines on topographic maps that trace zones of equal elevation. For a long time the isolines on many maps were referred to as Halleyan lines.

In 1687, the year he was wrapping up Newton's book, Halley published a study on the evaporation of seawater by the Sun. He deduced that there must be a gradual increase in the salinity of the oceans, a fact that suggested to him a possible way to measure the age of the Earth. And it seemed to him, by this measure, that the Earth must be much older than had been assumed on the basis of genealogical calculations derived from the Bible. His modern biographer, Colin Ronan, calls this "one of the earliest rational and scientific approaches" to the question of the Earth's age, even though the method never proved to be reliable. This would get him into some trouble with the ecclesiastical establishment. In 1691, he was refused a professorship at Oxford because of suspicions of his religious apostasy. Some called him a "banterer" of religion.

More than Halley could have known, he seems to have anticipated modern thinking that some of the Earth's most devastating catastrophes may have been caused by too-close encounters with extraterrestrial bodies. Halley suggested, for example, that the Caspian Sea was gouged out by a comet impacting the Earth at the time of the Biblical Flood. A comet coming too close to Earth or hitting Earth, he said, might have been the disrupting force causing the Flood. In recent years, scientists have argued rather persuasively that a meteorite or comet struck the Earth 65 million years ago and triggered a chain reaction of worldwide devastation. This, according to the hypothesis, caused the mass extinction of life at that time, dooming among other creatures the fabulous dinosaurs. Similar visitations, it is further postulated, may be responsible for what appears to be a pattern of mass extinctions occurring every 26 million years, the most recent event having happened 15 million years ago.

In 1688, Halley's ranging mind dealt with such matters as the phenomenon of heat, a fern he had observed on St. Helena, comparisons of English, French, and ancient Roman weights and measures, and some fossilized sea shells. The shells were found on the cliffs of Harwich, which, he said in a report, "seemed to demonstrate that that bed had once been the bottom of the sea, notwithstanding its being so much above it now." Few scientists of his day could bring themselves to accept such evidence of a past in which the world was perhaps much different from what it is now. It would be another century before they did, giving rise to modern geology and paleontology.

As an accomplished mathematician, Halley liked to experiment with calculations of a practical nature. One of his papers was "The Manner of Computing the Weight and Force of the Winds." He sought to determine the height to which bullets could be shot. Drawing on the records of the age and sex of all persons who died in Breslau during 1692, Halley computed the first sophisticated annuity tables for determining life-insurance payments. This influenced the future development of all actuarial tables.

Halley had a sense of adventure, too. Not only had he commanded a warship, but he climbed a mountain with a barometer to find out how the pressure of the air diminishes with altitude. He invented a diving bell and, in the summer of 1691 off the coast of Sussex, descended to test it himself. His unpublished paper on the invention was titled, "A Method of Walking Under Water."

Finally, Halley turned his attention again to the question of cometary paths. It was 1695.

The task, as he said, required an "immense labour." Halley calculated the path of twenty-four comets observed at different times, including the 1680 and 1682 comets. He consulted Newton's observations of the 1680 comet as well as his own notes made in Paris. He became convinced that comets traveled elliptical paths. Writing to Newton, with reference to his reanalysis of the 1680 comet that had so frustrated him as a younger man, Halley said: "I find certain indication of an Elliptick Orb in that Comet and am satisfied that it will be very difficult to hitt it exactly by a Parabolick."

By then Halley was also becoming convinced that the 1682 comet, the one he had observed at Islington, appeared to be the same as others seen in 1531 and 1607. The three comets called attention to themselves because they traveled the "wrong" way around the Sun—that is, they traveled in a direction opposite to that in which all the planets orbit. All three seemed to follow similar courses as they plunged in toward the Sun. Halley decided that he needed more detailed data on the 1682 comet before he could make up his mind, and the best information he knew was in the hands of Flamsteed, at Greenwich. But the two men were not on speaking terms. Halley, therefore, appealed to Newton in a letter to "procure for me of Mr Flamsteed what he has observed of the Comett of 1682 particularly in the month of September, for I am more and more confirmed that we have seen that Comett now three times, since Yeare 1531."

Newton got the data from Flamsteed and passed it on to Halley, who found it exceedingly valuable. This led Halley to conclude that the 1682 comet had also traveled an elliptical path. By these new calculations Halley determined that the elliptical path took the comet nearly 3.5 billion miles away from the Sun and then back again. He repeated his sums time and again, always getting the same answer.

**Edmond Halley at the age of eighty.** *(The Royal Society)*

Then Halley sought to connect the 1682 comet with those of 1607 and 1531. There was one slight problem. The time between the passing of the comet in 1531 and in 1607 was seventy-six years, and the time between 1607 and 1682 was only seventy-five years. How could this discrepancy be explained? Recalling some research he had done as a university student, which concerned Jupiter and Saturn, Halley surmised that the difference in the return times of the comet could be attributed to perturbations on its course caused by the gravity of the two huge planets. If on a particular return the comet came close to Jupiter or Saturn, their gravity would slow it down enough to throw it somewhat behind its predicted schedule.

Looking ahead, Halley sought to calculate when the comet should return to sight again. It was no easy matter. But it had great scientific import, even beyond the study of comets. There could be no more compelling proof of a scientific law than to predict events by means of it, and this was the first attempt to apply Newton's law of universal gravitation to a specific astronomical problem. For in making the calculations for his prediction, Halley had to take into account the positions of Jupiter and Saturn and the Earth and where the comet should be in relation to these three bodies. It was not until 1705 that Halley felt sure enough of his calculations to publish a prediction. In *A Synopsis of the Astronomy of Comets*, Halley wrote:

> Now many things lead me to believe that the comet in year 1531, observed by Apian, is the same as that which in the year 1607 was described by Kepler and Longomontanus, and which I myself saw and observed at its return in 1682. All the elements agree, except that there is an inequality in the times of revolution; but this is not so great that it cannot be attributed to physical causes. For example, the motion of Saturn is so disturbed by

the other planets, and especially by Jupiter, that its periodic time is uncertain to the extent of several days.

How much more liable to such perturbations is a comet which recedes to a distance nearly four times greater than that to Saturn, and a slight increase in whose velocity could change its orbit from an ellipse into a parabola! The identity of these comets is confirmed by the fact that in 1456 a comet was seen, which passed in a retrograde direction between the earth and the sun, in nearly the same manner; and although it was not observed astronomically, yet from its period and its path I infer that it was the same comet as that of the years 1531, 1607, and 1682. I may, therefore, with confidence predict its return in the year 1758. If this prediction is fulfilled, there is no reason to doubt that other comets will return.

Halley then appealed to future astronomers to watch the skies to see if his prediction came true. It was unlikely, he realized, that he would live to 1758 to see the comet again. But, if he was correct, he wanted to be remembered. In a later edition of *Synopsis*, published after his death, Halley expressed the hope that "candid posterity will not refuse to acknowledge that this was first discovered by an Englishman."

He could not have wished for greater acknowledgment. The Englishman Halley's name is now synonymous with comets, certainly with the comet that is more celebrated than all the others. The only dispute, it seems, has to do with the spelling of his first name and the pronunciation of his family name. So often the first name is spelled Edmund. But in his will he declared: "In the name of God, I Edmond Halley . . ." Edmond it should be. But agreement on pronunciation of the last name is harder to arrive at.

In his 1980 book *The Comet Is Coming,* Nigel Calder reviewed the three main possibilities:

Ha'li rhyming with alley, the obvious one for anyone accustomed to the peculiarities of English spelling. Ha'li rhyming with bailey, often preferred by those who grew up with the pop group known as Bill Haley and the Comets. Ho'li rhyming with bawley, favoured by Colin Ronan, one of Halley's biographers, on the grounds that the astronomer's name was sometimes spelt Hawley; but then it was also spelt Haley or Halley, on occasions.

We telephoned sixteen Halleys living in London to ask them what they called themselves. Three declined to say but every one of the remainder admitted to Ha'li (rhyming with alley), although one respondent mentioned a brother who called himself Ha'li (rhyming with bailey). With such an overwhelming verdict about the present pronunciation of the name there was no point in continuing the survey. . . .

Judging by the way his contemporaries spelled the name, any of the pronunciations could apply. At a meeting in London of the Halley's Comet Society in 1983, as reported in *The New Yorker* magazine, Brian Harpur, the society's founder and honorary secretary, introduced "impeccable historical evidence" from no less than Queen Anne to support the Hawley pronunciation. "She spelt his name 'H-a-w-l-e-y,'" Harpur declared. "Furthermore, the flower arrangement you may have admired when you arrived was most excellently contrived for us by a Mrs. Halley, spelt 'H-a-l-l-e-y,' pronounced 'Hawley'." There were cheers and more toasts from the Hawley partisans. In various other accounts by contemporaries, the name was spelled (and so presumably pronounced) Hailey, Haley, Halley, Haly, Hawley, Hawly, and Hayley. And so it will probably go, Halley alley, Halley bailey, Halley bawley, as the name falls from the lips of countless people when the comet comes around again. For what it is worth, Michael Belton, an English-born astronomer at the

Kitt Peak National Observatory in Arizona, says, "I urge that we stick with 'Hal-ly'."

Halley, as he expected, did not live to 1758, the predicted time of the comet's return. In his latter years, he became the Astronomer Royal, succeeding Flamsteed, and continued to busy himself with a wide variety of scientific interests and concern himself with the affairs of the Royal Society. To the end he was a sociable man. He founded the Royal Society Club, a group of his close scientist friends who met weekly to eat and drink and talk. Although in 1737 he suffered a slight stroke, which left him partially paralyzed in his right hand, he rarely missed the club's Thursday dinners till within a short time of his death. He was sitting in his chair at the Greenwich Observatory when the end came on January 14, 1742, in the eighty-sixth year of his life. He poured himself a glass of wine, took a long drink, and quietly passed away.

Soon after Halley's death, three French astronomers refined Halley's calculations and issued even more precise predictions on the time and position of the comet as it made its way through the inner Solar System in late 1758 and early 1759. As the time approached, astronomers throughout Europe strained to be the first to see the comet that Halley had promised them, or to bear the news that Halley had been wrong.

One of these astronomers was Charles Messier, the first of a special breed of sky watchers known as comet hunters. He spent most of his active life as a clerk and observer at the Paris Observatory. People called him the Ferret because of his uncanny ability to track down new comets. Comet hunting was, then as now, a competitive occupation. By the time Messier had twelve discoveries to his name, he was forced to interrupt his searches to care for his sick wife, during which time a rival, Montaigne of Limoges, discovered a new comet. At his wife's fu-

neral, Messier is said to have forgotten his wife
completely, thinking only of the comet he had
missed. Responding to one offer of condolence, Messier lamented, "Alas, Montaigne has robbed me of
my thirteenth comet."

A reward for all the long, sleepless nights of comet
hunting is to have one's name recorded in the annals
of astronomy. The customary practice is to name a
new comet for its discoverer or discoverers; often,
two or three people make independent and simultaneous sightings. In a few cases, such as Halley's, a
comet bears the name not of its discoverer but of the
scientist who computed its orbit. So it is with
Comet Crommelin. The comet was discovered in
1818 by Jean-Louis Pons, a one-time janitor at the
Marseilles Observatory who became an inveterate
comet hunter. The same comet was seen again in
1873 and 1928, but each time it was assumed to be a
newly discovered body and so was given a new
name. Finally, Andrew C. D. Crommelin, an astronomer at the Greenwich Observatory, determined
that all those sightings had been of the same comet
and predicted its reappearance in 1956. By then the
name of the comet (which, in a sense, had four discoverers) had been changed to Crommelin by the
International Astronomical Union, following a deci-
sion to limit comet designations to the names of no
more than three codiscoverers. The convention of
naming comets has been modified again in recent
years to reflect a new development in astronomy,
the discovery of comets not by people but by spacecraft. In 1983, the Infrared Astronomical Satellite
(IRAS) discovered five new comets, the most prominent of which was duly named IRAS-Araki-Alcock.
The latter were amateur astronomers, Genichi Araki
in Japan and George Alcock in England, who first
photographed the comet using backyard telescopes.

Amateurs are usually the most indefatigable
comet hunters. As Patrick Moore, the British astron-

**Andrew C. D. Crommelin.**

omer and writer, has noted, comet hunting is attractive to amateurs because it does not require really
powerful telescopes; what comet hunters need is a
wide field of view and only moderate magnification,
which means that powerful, well-mounted binoculars are ideal.

Comet hunting also takes patience, uncommon
patience. Rodney Austin in New Zealand, an amateur, searched the skies for fourteen years before he

made his first comet discovery in 1982. While most professionals have their sights set on grander vistas, the galaxies and quasars and nebular clouds, the amateurs spend hour after hour at night in the hope of finding a dim new comet making its way in toward the Sun. Alcock, an English schoolmaster, is a typical practitioner. Using a pair of mounted binoculars, he has discovered several comets, two of them sighted within one week. Kaoru Ikeya built his own telescope and looked for comets night after night for years in Japan, to win some fame and thus clear his family's name of the shame brought about by the father's failures. His discoveries were many in the 1960s, including the conspicuous Ikeya-Seki comet of 1965. Tsutomu Seki was another amateur, a teacher of classical guitar. Among the other highly successful amateur comet hunters of recent years are Charles Bradfield in Australia, Jack Bennett in South Africa, and Leslie Peltier in the United States. The clearinghouse for comet discoveries, by amateurs and professionals alike, is at the Smithsonian Astrophysical Observatory in Cambridge, Massachusetts, where Brian Marsden receives, reviews, and publicizes the reports of cometary comings and goings.

A few of the amateurs graduated to professional status. Pons, for example, did not remain an observatory janitor forever; he rose to the rank of observatory director. Edward Barnard, one of the foremost American comet hunters at the turn of the century, was a photographer and was the first to discover a comet using a photograph of the night sky. In time he moved from comets to a celebrated career observing the stars, one of which now bears his name.

There have been many comets and many comet hunters before and since, but never was there a greater sense of anticipation among comet hunters than in the waning days of 1758. Edmond Halley was long dead. But everyone in science remembered his prediction. Soon, as the comet hunters would see, "candid posterity" would have reason to remember his name and discovery that comets can return to be seen again and again with predictable regularity.

# THREE

# The Early History

**Or, Why All the Fuss?**

*The trilling wire in the blood*
*Sings below inveterate scars*
*And reconciles forgotten wars.*
*The dance along the artery*
*The circulation of the lymph*
*Are figured in the drift of stars. . . .*

—T. S. ELIOT,
"Burnt Norton," *Four Quartets*

On the night of Christmas 1758, a German farmer and amateur astronomer named Johann Georg Palitzsch became the first person to spot a comet whose return had been predicted. Edmond Halley was right. Here it was. The comet he had said would reappear did in fact reappear. He did not live to see it. But here in the sky near Dresden was the most important comet in history. Forever after, Comet Halley.

In the first few weeks it did not look like much. But by the middle of March, after it had reached perihelion, the closest approach to the Sun its orbit would allow, it had become a brilliant nightly spectacle with a tail stretching a quarter of the way across the night sky.

What was happening in those months of 1759 was far more than just an exciting bit of comet gazing for a coterie of amateur and professional astronomers. This was an age when people still generally believed that comets were the work of wild and mighty, often terrifying and angry, celestial forces, an age when common people and intellectuals alike were only just beginning to understand the exquisite design of physical forces subsequently perceived to be at work in the universe. So the realization that a comet had appeared in the heavens at a time predicted by man, that it must have approached the Earth on a clock-work basis for centuries and would no doubt go on doing so indefinitely struck with the majesty of a great bronze gong sounding through the theater of man's collective imagination.

Here now in the simple appearance of a single comet was the pristine proof of the elaborate and once dangerously radical theories of Copernicus, Galileo, Tycho Brahe, Kepler, Newton, and Edmond Halley.

But if the appearance of Halley's Comet was an important validation of the scientific revolution of the seventeenth century, it had other implications as well. At once, it cast a light into the final shadows of the Dark Ages and helped illuminate the dawning age of Enlightenment. The new understanding of the universe—an understanding based on astrophysics and mathematical equation—would reverberate through the rationalist, liberal, humanitarian, and scientific trends of the eighteenth century, and on into the industrial and technical revolutions as well. At the very least the eighteenth-century thinker was now forced again, as his ancestors had been in the earlier two centuries with the great oceanic explorations, to reevaluate man's own relationship to himself and to the space around him. The cosmos could now be viewed both with a great deal less respect and a great deal more.

Thus, the transformation from the past was profound. Little had been known about the comet until the seventeenth century. Only the drama was clear, time and again: The appearances of Halley's Comet, before the days of Kepler and Copernicus, were pure fire and brimstone. Out of the darkness hurtled this fireball with tail stretching far across the sky. Must it not have been hurled by some angry god as punishment for man's transgressions? And would it not scorch the very earth if it hit? And even if it didn't, was there any doubt that certain unfathomable celestial forces were in full control of man's fate?

This comet has, down through the centuries, been associated with more nonscientific fuss and excitement, more awe and admiration, more hoopla and chicanery—indeed, more outright misery, fear, death, and destruction—than any other innocent, peaceful floating ball of ice and dust in the galaxy.

Perhaps the single most important myth about the comet was that it had the power to precipitate great, often terrible events. Pestilence, plague, fame, fortune, fraud, the wrath of the gods, the anger of popes, the fear of kings, the weeping and the wailing of the peoples from the steppes of Russia to the streets of Greenwich Village—all have been tied to Halley's Comet. Every seventy-six years or so, at least since 240 B.C. and probably well before that, the excitement in many ways has been much the same.

The comet has played roles in religion, in military thinking, in literature and art and in plain old superstition down through the ages. As with the best of myths and some of the best of lies, there has always been a bit of truth embedded in the beliefs. They start with a few facts and then let the tale go where it will. Even now, the known truths about the comet are still couched in enough ignorance to leave plenty of room for creative conjecture.

The creativity of the past often was fueled by coincidence. A string of absolutely stunning coincidences have accompanied Halley's Comet throughout time. It was, for instance, Halley's Comet, beyond doubt, that finally brought down poor old Methuselah. The Biblical figure managed to do just fine for 969 years. But then, as British astronomer Sir Robert Hall calculated at the turn of this century, the comet appeared in 2616 B.C., and that was it for Methuselah. (By the extended logic of this theory, Methuselah would have withstood the comet's fury twelve times during his 969 years. It must have been the thirteenth return that got him!)

---

## The Comet in Religion

Probably the clearest influence of the comet has been on religious belief, the comet's seeming to serve often as a reminder of the existence of otherworldly power. Here for the believers and the skeptics alike was positive evidence of the existence of the supernatural. Or at least the extraterrestrial. Before the twentieth century, before the Wright brothers, before the exploration of interplanetary and then interstellar space, the notions and explanations of the extraterrestrial behavior were pretty much the same: Divine forces determined what appeared where and when. Thus, an unknown object appearing unexpectedly in the night sky was big theological news and, generally speaking, probably not good theological news.

Some scholars contend that the writer or writers of I Chronicles in the Old Testament were of the opinion that a comet—which, in retrospect, these scholars maintain, must have been Halley's—slashed across the sky like a sword as a warning from God to King David for conducting an illegal census.

A comet—almost certainly Halley's—was said to have slashed across the sky like a sword as a warning from God to King David. That sword, as depicted here, appeared as the weapon of an angel. *(The Bettmann Archive)*

And God was displeased with this thing: therefore He smote Israel. . . .

And God sent an angel unto Jerusalem to destroy it. . . . And the angel of the Lord stood by the threshing floor of Ornan the Jebusite.

And David lifted up his eyes, and saw the angel

of the Lord stand between the earth and heaven,
having a drawn sword in his hand stretched out
over Jerusalem.

I Chronicles, Chapter 21

The phrase "a drawn sword in his hand stretched
out over Jerusalem," a sword held up "between the
earth and heaven," is a reference—according to
some astronomers calculating possible appearances
of the comet—to Halley's tail. As a mere youth,
David took on Goliath with reckless abandon, but
he was not about to challenge the comet. "Afraid of
the sword of the angel of the Lord," he repented and
procured the land of Ornan the Jebusite for a magnificent temple.

Dr. Gunnar Norlung, writing in the *Journals of
the British Astronomical Association* (Vol. 65, No. 7
[July 1955], pp. 285–89), says his research indicated
that the comet returned about the year 1005 B.C.,
which may have been right about the time of David's troubles over the census. Dr. Norlung concedes
that, since Ornan himself saw the angel while
threshing wheat, the incident must have taken place
in broad daylight. So the comet must have been a
daylight comet, and one of considerable size and
brilliance. Daylight sightings have indeed been reported. Halley's Comet was seen over Africa in
1910, for instance, and the Chinese recorded sighting a brilliant, full daylight comet on September 9,
1222.

Some remain skeptical of the Norlung theory, the
British astronomer David A. Seargent among them.
Seargent points out that Halley's Comet would have
to be of much greater intrinsic brightness than it actually is to have glowed in daylight over Ornan's
wheat field with the kind of brilliance I Chronicles
describes. "It is difficult to see how it could have
been this brilliant," Seargent writes in *Comets: Vagabonds of Space*. Halley's is much farther from the

Sun at perihelion than the brightest of the daytime comets, he points out, adding that

> its light is not from glowing metallic elements evaporated from dust particles under the fierce heat of the sun. . . . An extremely high intrinsic magnitude (or, brightness) would be implied, and this in turn would imply a large-scale fading since the time of David. Also, the sword seems to have been of secondary importance. The main "vision" concerned the angel—described in clearly anthropomorphic terms—and it is difficult to see how a comet could be mistaken for a man.

But if the comet were not the Lord himself in phantasmagoria, or even a surrogate angel, the fireball-hurled-by-God belief persisted for centuries. Accordingly, Halley's appearance in 837 so frightened Louis I, the Emperor of France and Germany, that he ordered the construction of many more churches and monasteries.

The comet's truest moment of religious glory may have come with its appearance in a Nativity scene as the star of Bethlehem heralding the birth of Christ and the founding of Christianity. This association, however, appears to be more imaginative than factual.

There is no actual historical or scientific evidence that Halley's Comet returned on the night Christ was born. Reconstructions made after Edmond Halley discovered the comet's periodicity place its closest returns to the birth of Christ at 11 B.C. and A.D. 66. But a substantial body of tradition in the Middle Ages associated the star of Bethlehem with a comet. So it is not surprising that Halley's showed up in the frescoes painted by the Florentine master Giotto di Bondone on the walls of the Scrovegni Chapel in Padua. Scholars agree that Giotto probably saw the comet in the late summer of 1301 when it appeared in the night sky. Soon thereafter, perhaps within the

The comet (top, center) appeared in Giotto's depiction of the
birth of Christ in the Scrovegni Chapel.

year or at least not more than within four years, he completed the chapel frescoes, depicting the Adoration of the Magi. Roberta J. M. Olson pointed out in *Scientific American* (May 1979, p. 160) that Giotto encouraged his viewers to identify with the miraculous event of Christ's birth, and that the painting's emotional intensity is heightened by the presence of the comet, dominating the sky, pulsating with energy, intense light, and long trailing tail. Moreover, many of the viewers, too, had seen the comet. Thus, for them, it became associated—if 1,300 years after the fact—with the founding of their Church and the initiation of the central religious force of their lives.

The founding of the Christian Church aside, the comet has always had—and perhaps always will have—spiritual connotations. Any clear starlit night has the power to bathe the spirit. And an evening on which Halley's Comet has appeared has never been an ordinary starlit night. Down through the centuries, through generations, seen once in a lifetime, it seemed more the perfect link with time present and time past. And time future, as T. S. Eliot said, contained in time past. In short, the beauty, the mystery, the awe, all combining in the mystical or deeply religious personal experience that for so many has by itself been enough to sustain the comet in the echoes of memory.

*The Comet at War* Balm to the spirit though it may have been, this comet has had its share of bellicose moments as well. The suspected military might of Halley's Comet was every bit as great as the belief in its religious significance.

It is blamed, though mostly in hindsight, for the war that ended with the destruction of Jerusalem in A.D. 66, for the attack on the Ostrogoths by the

Huns in 373, the invasion of Gaul by Attila in 451, the colonization of America by the English after 1607. The vulnerable old comet has even been blamed for the end of French power in America with the fall of Quebec in 1759. Halley's worst collaboration appears to have been with Genghis Khan. He thought the comet was his own special star, and as it made its grand appearance in 1222, his Mongol armies pushing toward southeast Europe massacred millions of people in the cities of Herat and Samarkand, and other areas.

The comet with an unfailing flair for the dramatic managed to turn up in the one year whose date is known to every English-speaking schoolchild, 1066, the Norman Conquest. In that year, Halley's was taken by the Saxons on the one hand as an omen of defeat and by William the Conqueror as "a wonderful sign from Heaven." He pointed to the comet appearing nightly as the war raged to spur his invading Norman soldiers on to victory. Thus, to the extent that the mass psychology of a people affects their waging of war, the comet played a true role in the outcome of this war and, through it, the course of political history.

It has been asserted by some that, during wartime, Pope Calixtus III went so far as to excommunicate Halley's Comet in 1456 as a fraudulent, un-Christian heretic. Others contend that what he really did was ask that God protect the Christians from "the devil, the Turks and the comet." The reference to the Turks was an allusion to a bloody fight. The Turks were threatening Europe. They had captured Constantinople and were now turning on Belgrade. Scientists later confirmed that Halley's Comet did appear at a crucial stage in the war and brightly lighted up the night over the battle of Belgrade. The Europeans, believing the comet foretold disaster, could not decide what to fear more, the Turks or the comet. As history shows, the Turks won the battle.

Subsequently, however, they were defeated, and Europe was saved. Whether it was because the menacing comet had now headed back out to the harmless reaches of the Solar System, or because of the pope's intercession or other factors, is, of course, not known.

***Superstition*** Science has never been entirely free of superstition,
***in Science*** and comets have often gotten all tangled up in the confusion.

Some of the earliest science—and superstition—involving comets occurred some 4,000 years ago in China. The emperors of China retained staffs of astronomers and astrologers to keep a constant watch on the Moon, Sun, stars, planets, and comets, believing all imperial power stemmed from the relative positions these objects assumed in the sky. The knowledge acquired was regarded as top secret because it was thought to be invaluable as a fatal weapon in the hands of enemies of the empire. Actually, as Nigel Calder writes in *The Comet Is Coming*, the Chinese invented clocks, to operate armillaries that would represent the motion of planets and stars, out of consideration of the imperial sex life. "It was essential," he says, "to know the precise configuration of the sky at the time of conception of a prince, so that the prognoses could be made, and with their cunning machinery, the astrologers could allow events in the imperial bedchamber to take their course on the cloudiest of nights." The stargazing business was taken with utter seriousness by the Chinese. According to one legend, two astronomers, Hi and Ho, were once found so drunk on the job that they failed to notice even an eclipse of the Sun. The emperor cut off their heads.

In medieval Europe, when Halley's Comet would

appear, kings and serfs called on the local astrologer to tell them what it portended and how to guard against its ill effects. Superstitious maybe. But these were not necessarily unintelligent folk. The founder of modern astronomy, after all, was among them. Johannes Kepler, who evolved the laws of planetary motion that enabled Edmond Halley to make his prediction in 1682, made his living as, of all things, a court astrologer for Emperor Rudolf II. Astrologers were not apt to attribute the origin of comets to the vindictive behavior of angry gods. Rather, they saw them as evolving from the conjunction of the planets in one of the signs of the zodiac. But they too believed that comets were omens or foretold the future in some way, and it was their job to interpret them by studying their position relative to the Moon, Sun, and stars.

Not long before Edmond Halley was born, Johannes Kepler, with the aid of the earlier work and later collaboration of Tycho Brahe, his teacher, brilliantly determined the paths of planets. He discovered that they apparently orbit in an ellipse, of which the Sun's center is one of the foci, that the radius vector of each planet—that is, the line that could be drawn to join its center with that of the Sun —moves over equal areas in equal times, and that the square of the period of each planet's revolution around the Sun is proportional to the cube of its mean distance from the Sun. So it was ultimately Kepler, as well as Newton and Halley, whose work the German farmer was validating on that Christmas night in 1758.

Still, even Kepler accepted the notion that comets were evil omens. Seymour L. Chapin writes in a bulletin of the Astronomical Society of the Pacific (*Leaflet No. 278*, June 1952) that Kepler did not believe comets were subject to his new planetary laws, and Galileo believed much the same thing.

Descartes, however, was another matter. He insisted they were natural phenomena. But Descartes was a philosopher not an astronomer. Still, Descartes was greatly respected in other fields, and surprising as it was that he should be challenging both Galileo and Kepler in their own space, so to speak, his views did represent one of the first large cracks in the myths surrounding Comet Halley. Another is attributable to Seth Ward, a professor of astronomy at Oxford. Having examined the appearances of a comet in 1652, Professor Ward decided that the comet must revolve around the Sun in either extremely eccentric circles or in ellipses, which could either include or exclude the Earth. Ward is credited with being the first to conceive the idea of comets having regulated orbits, though others may have thought of it independently.

***. . . And Among the Literati*** Galileo Galilei and Kepler were never alone in their superstition, however. If there is somewhere—say on Planet X, the suspected tenth planet—a gallery of great figures, mythic themselves, who hung on to superstition about Halley's Comet, Mark Twain is among them. And James Thurber might be there, too. Though Twain and Thurber would probably insist now that they were just taking some literary license. The biographer Albert Bigelow Paine wrote that, in 1909, Twain, afflicted with a series of heart attacks, said, "I came in with Halley's Comet in 1835. It is coming again next year, and I expect to go out with it. It will be the greatest disappointment of my life if I don't. The Almighty has said, no doubt: 'Now here are these two unaccountable freaks; they came in together, they must go out together.' Oh, I am looking forward to that."

Twain got his wish. The comet's brightest moment in the sun—perihelion—occurred on April 20, 1910. Twain died the next day.

As for Thurber, he calmly pointed out that he was never worried about the comet's 1910 appearance. "Nothing happened," he said, "except that I was left with a curious twitching of my left ear after sundown and a tendency to break into a dog trot at the striking of a match or the flashing of a lantern."

Another reason for the long run of excitement surrounding comets has been that they have always had a good press, or perhaps just good literary agents, in the sense that it doesn't matter how writers damage reputations in print as long as the names are spelled right. Clearly what was going on with Twain and Thurber was that as great writers they knew great material when they saw it. Natural phenomena are principal reference materials for writer and artist, and the image could scarcely be resisted. Once observed, comets would now appear again and again in their imaginations as points of comparison, and appear again and again in their works as metaphors. Early on, the comet was the villain. In *Paradise Lost*, Milton associates the libel-proof comet with an enraged Satan and, ultimately, with pestilence and war:

> *Incenst with indignation Satan stood*
> *Unterrifi'd, and like a Comet burn'd,*
> *That fires the length of Ophiuchus huge*
> *In th' Artick Sky, and from his horrid hair*
> *Shakes Pestilence and Warr.*

You wonder if Milton wasn't above lifting a line or two from Homer. In the *Iliad* Homer writes that Achilles' helmet shone

> *Like the red star, that from his flaming hair*
> *Shakes down disease, pestilence, and war.*

Milton, though blind when he wrote *Paradise Lost*, had seen the comet of 1618 as a child, and was

no doubt calling upon his own imagination as well.
English literature scholars believe he was almost
certainly referring to a 1618 comet, which, inciden-
tally, John Evelyn's *Diary* blames for the great
Thirty Years War in Europe, which broke out that
same year: ". . . the effects of that Comet, still working in the prodigious revolutions now beginning in
Europe, especially in Germany." The 1618 comet
was in the constellation Ophiuchus, specifically
mentioned in the Milton passage. It was a striking
object with one of the longest tails ever recorded—
104 degrees, that is one that stretched more than
halfway across the night sky and probably made a
great impression on Milton, and the impression
lasted a lifetime. But it was not a lifetime happy association. By the time Milton wrote those lines in
*Paradise Lost* in 1684 three other comets had appeared, and conventional wisdom blamed them for
the English war with the Dutch and for the Plague of
London.

It would be wrong to contend that Halley's got
only a bad press. *Punch*, for example, in 1910, said
this:

> No more I feel the potent spell
> of Jupiter or Mars,
> Or know the magic peace that fell
> Upon me from the Stars,
> A fiercer flame—a Comet Love
> Consumes my spirit now;
> I cry to you in heavens above,
> "Oh! Halley's, where are thou!"

Indeed, in *Julius Caesar* Shakespeare saw the
bright side:

> When beggars die, there are no comets seen;
> The heavens themselves blaze forth the death of
> princes.

And the contemporary novelist John Calvin
Batchelor went from the lugubrious to the delight-
fully comic in *The Further Adventures of Halley's
Comet*, in which a sinister, American-based multi-
national—well, perhaps multicelestial—corporation schemed elaborately to seize control of Halley's
Comet and use it as their ultimate, sinister secret
weapon for the conquest of the universe. Only two
brave New York stockbrokers and their ancient
friends, who, by the way, only appeared on Earth at
times of crisis, every seventy-six years, managed to
save the day for justice and humanity.

Halley's in the art world, however, has been,
except for occasional drawings in *Punch* or by
Daumier, the indomitable French caricaturist, a serious matter. The comet's artistic place, as with its
religious place, was, as pointed out earlier, really affirmed by Giotto, the father of naturalist painting.
His depiction of the comet in the Scrovegni Chapel
was a dramatic departure from the iconographic tradition of a stylized many-pointed little star. That
tradition never varied greatly from the oldest known
drawing of the comet: a thin line sketch, published
in the Nürnberg Chronicles, of Halley's appearance
in A.D. 684. (Accompanying text says the comet
brought on three months of rain, thunder, and light-
ning; people and flocks died, it says, grain withered,
and a plague followed an eclipse both of the Sun and
the Moon.) Giotto, on the other hand, painted the
comet as he really saw it: a blazing, speeding object
of great beauty and energy, and not after all dissimi-
lar to the actual photographs taken of the comet in
1910.

The first contemporaneous portrait—though one
that conforms, in its re-creation of the comet, far
more to the artistic style of the medieval tapestry
than to any sense of excitement, fear, or wonder, as
Giotto's seemed to have—was commissioned by
Queen Matilda, the wife of William the Conqueror,

to illustrate her husband's victory in 1066 over King Harold at the Battle of Hastings. The work, which is actually a crewel embroidery, is 231 feet long by 19½ feet wide and hangs in the town hall of Bayeux in Normandy. If the artist didn't help further the myth of Halley's power, the caption writer, in his reference to the watchers below, did. "They are," the tapestry legend said, "in awe of the star."

The Padua of northern Italy where Giotto mixed art and religion provided a natural conjunction of art and science as well. It was a center of mathematics, a field of knowledge that, basically, led Newton to his laws of gravitation, Tycho Brahe and Kepler to planetary motion, and Halley to his understanding of comets. It is no accident that, by Giotto's time, scholars in his city had begun to study the heavens assiduously. That tradition lasted. Galileo taught at the University of Padua—though that was 300 years later.

*Pure Science and Pure Chicanery* But lest we unbalance the history of Halley's Comet, it is important to stress that the search for natural, physical truths has been, in many ways, just as responsible for the interest in Halley's Comet, particularly during the later centuries, as all the other causes. Superstition, fear of the unknown, religious faith—all were key factors. But interest in the pursuit of science was essential to the public's interest in the comet as well.

But, judging from what happened in 1910, the myths will not entirely vanish either. For despite 400 years of culminating science, despite the advances in telescopic observation in communication made possible by the development of the wireless, the clouds of misinformation and myth surrounding Halley's Comet seemed as thick as ever. And there was silliness and chicanery, too.

In 1066, the comet (top, center) was seen as "a wonderful sign from Heaven" by William the Conqueror and as an omen of defeat by the Saxons. The crewel embroidery, which is 231 by 19½ feet and hangs in Bayeux, was commissioned by Queen Matilda, wife of William the Conqueror, to illustrate his victory. *(The Bettmann Archive)*

Early on April 29, 1910, on the main street of Towaco, New Jersey, two young, well-dressed men
appeared as a kind of *Good Morning America*, reporting that a particularly splendid view of the returning Halley's Comet could be seen that night
from the top of nearby Waukhaw Mountain. This,
they said, would be the astronomical spectacle of a
lifetime. The scientific event of the century. Indeed,
in an attempt to kindle a general interest in science,
the technology institute they represented, they said,
was offering prizes for the best amateur description
of the comet and its long tail as they appeared in the
night sky. A young woman named Lily—described
by a raconteur of the time as the more than talented
daughter of one Cyrus Lautergan—was first to accept the challenge, announcing that she would be at
the mountaintop with palette and easel. A rival
popped up. Mary Vanderlip was quick to point out,
however, that, as far as sky coloring was concerned,
she was equal and most likely superior to Lily Lautergan. Mary would most definitely be there, too.

"Well, anyway," *The New York Times* reported
the following morning, "this morning Waukhaw
Mountain top was covered with Towaco's beauty
and chivalry and chaperonage. Miss Lily and Miss
Mary were ready with their palettes, with bets on
the winner." But in the end the night was less than a
success. Not only did fog and clouds obscure Halley's Comet, but when the good citizens of Towaco
returned to their homes, they found that their
chicken coops had been looted. Cyrus Doolite lost
300 fowls, and the Lautergan and Vanderlip families
were heavy losers as well.

"Halley's comet can go to the dickens, as far as
I'm concerned," said Mr. Lautergan, after he counted
his losses. "Doggone comets anyhow."

In 1910, though, the comet had taken on such
an ominous mien, for some, that a bit of looting
amounted to little. Its clouds were said to contain

deadly poisonous gas. Cyrus Lautergan's stolen chickens were nothing. Wasn't the world about to pass right through the tail of the comet? Were not distinguished astronomers in distinguished observatories being reported in distinguished newspapers as saying that cyanogen gas left in the wake of the famous comet would impregnate the world's atmosphere and snuff out life on the planet?

Perhaps T. S. Eliot was right. Destiny was being figured in the drift of stars, after all. Perhaps this was the end.

# F O U R

# 1910:
# Will the
# Earth Survive?

**Fear Takes Over** If science had taken the mystery out of comets by 1910, if knowledge had dispelled fear, if hard facts had cleared away the mists of myth, you couldn't tell it in Chicago. Indeed, a substantial portion of the people of the world had a pretty good case of the jitters, as Halley's Comet prepared to make its twenty-ninth appearance since generally accepted astronomical records had been kept. Who was to blame for all the nervousness and why it grew to the extent it did is hard to tell. Then as now scientists often placed the responsibility for such matters on the press, and the press tended to point to inaccurate or conflicting reports of scientists. There's probably enough blame to go around. Or maybe no one is to blame. It may be that this particular natural event can be—indeed, had often been—so awesome, so startling, that fear was inevitable. In any case, things got a bit out of hand.

On the morning of May 18, 1910, as Halley's Comet was about to reach its closest point to Earth, *The New York Times* reported in its lead story— page 1, right hand column—that that night the planet Earth would slice across the tail of the comet.

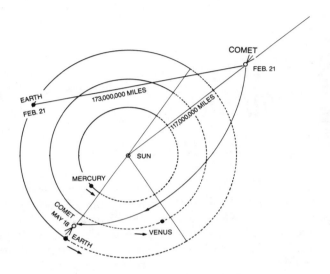

**The passage of Earth through the comet's tail in 1910 was cause for great alarm because of the widespread erroneous belief that poisonous gas in the comet's tail could do immeasurable damage.**

The Earth, *The Times* reported, would spend six hours in the comet's tail, traveling 1 "million miles, or 48 trillion cubic miles," through its trailing dust particles and gaseous substance. The account was based on the observations of the director of the Lick Observatory in California and others. Rumors and some scientific reports had circulated for months that the tail contained deadly cyanogen gas. The newspaper was careful to point out that the cyanogen gas was so rarefied that those 48 trillion cubic miles of material would weigh, all told, less than half an ounce, and therefore was so diffuse as to present no danger. Moreover, in an editorial the day before, the paper had said, "While it is true that what even the most learned of astronomers know about comets is probably less than what they have still to discover . . . . it is also true that they know enough to warrant their confident assurances that nobody need worry over the happenings of to-morrow night."

But Chicago, not to mention Paris, Bermuda, Johannesburg, and much of the rest of the world, was worried. In fact, reported *The Times*, Chicago was terrified. Especially, one is forced to conclude, the women. In the May 18 issue, it said:

> Terror occasioned by the near approach of Halley's comet has seized hold of a large part of the population of Chicago. Especially has the feminine portion succumbed. All else is forgotten. Comets and their ways and habits have been the principal topic discussed in the streets, cars, and elevated trains to-day. . . . The principal fear is not that the comet will strike the earth, but that the gas which it is supposed makes up the tail will wipe out all life. "I have stopped [up] all the windows and doors in my flat to keep the gas out," said one woman over the telephone. "All the other women in the building think it is a good thing, and all are doing the same." . . . Physicians say that there were scores of calls to-day for their services from women who were suffering from hysteria.

Nerves were taut in New York as well. Two nights before, the passengers in a streetcar traveling north on Eighth Avenue leaped to the street for safety because they thought Halley's Comet had hit the roof. "It's the comet!" one passenger screamed, and no one paused to disagree. But their fears of imminent death were at least premature. Though it was still too soon to know whether they would survive the cyanogen gas attack, their belief that they had been struck by the comet itself proved false. It

turned out that employees of a nearby fifth-floor motor company were testing a new cooling fan for automobiles when one of the blades of the fan let loose.
It flew through an open window and went hurtling
into what may now safely be called "lower space."
Lower-space experts of the day proclaimed that the
blade weighed about twenty pounds, that it had been
traveling at 1,000 RPM when it broke away, and that
it shot upward at least 600 feet before Newton's
"law of gravitation overcame the thrust of momentum and the blade started downward."

The downward shooting lower-space object stuck
in the roof of the car, and no one was hurt. Traffic
patrolman John Maine had caught a glimpse of the
fan blade as it fell and scanned the skies for a falling
airplane. His airplane theory was listed as the official exculpation of Halley's Comet until James Murray, an employee of the motor company, appeared at
the West Side precinct and put in a claim for the fan
blade.

What was happening in Chicago, what was happening in New York, what was happening elsewhere
as well at this time in May were all part of the whole
fascinating story of Halley's 1910 return. This story
really begins in the summer of the previous year,
then builds gradually to an almost deafening cre-
scendo. This visit of the vagabond comet, as Halley's
was being called in the late months of 1909 with
considerably less reverence than King David or Genghis Khan held for it, became as delightful, charm-
ing, maddening, and, yes, threatening, as ever.

By August of 1909, intense international rivalry
had developed among scientists of the major observatories of the world to recover—that is, make the
first sighting—of the comet. By then every major
telescope was sweeping the heavens for it. The leading contender was the Lick Observatory. Though
vastly weaker than the 1986 instruments trained on

Halley's Comet, the Lick telescope on Mount Hamilton was among the most powerful of its time, and, with it, astronomers there had discovered twelve comets. But the credit for recovering Halley's Comet went to the Germans. On September 11, 1909, elated observers at the Heidelberg Observatory reported sighting the comet.

In January 1910 a minor threat to Halley's celebrity appeared—a comet which came to be known as Comet A 1910, but which was at first mistaken for Halley's. In Mexico, special pilgrimages were being organized to the shrine of the Virgin of Talpa out of fear of Comet A. Because of this confusion, the comet that for centuries was so closely identified with the delusions of man or his significant developments in science was now losing some of its thunder, and critics of astrology and amateur astronomy were annoyed about the confusion. It was evidently one thing to accuse a comet falsely of fostering pestilence, war, and all else that went wrong with the world (or right with the world, for that matter: some believed that Halley's Comet was going to produce vintage wine in 1910). But it was quite another thing to accuse or pay homage to the wrong comet. Accordingly, what was probably the first call went out for some form of government regulation of space. Washington, the critics said, should officially record which comet is which and give each an official name.

Then on February 7, 1910, the centuries-old story of the comet, the story already so entangled with sincere belief, honest science, and utter balderdash, took what was in an important sense a far more serious turn. Astronomers at the Harvard Observatory reported that they had not yet made a photographic spectrum of Halley's Comet—that is, the real one—but that they had received a telegram from the Yerkes Observatory stating that its director and as-

**Comet A appeared in January of 1910 and was mistaken for the anxiously awaited Halley apparition.** *(Lick Observatory)*

sistants had determined that the comet contained bands of cyanogen gas. The story appeared on page 1 of *The New York Times* with this headline:

COMET'S POISONOUS TAIL
Yerkes Observatory Finds Cyanogen
in Spectrum of Halley's Comet

The article, under a Boston dateline and reporting Harvard's receipt of the Yerkes Observatory telegram, went on to describe the nature of the discovered gas: "Cyanogen is a very deadly poison, a grain of its potassium salt touched to the tongue being sufficient to cause instant death. In the uncombined state it is a bluish gas very similar in its chemical behavior to chlorine and extremely poisonous. It is characterized by an odor similar to that of almonds. The fact that cyanogen is present in the comet has been communicated to Camille Flammarion and many other astronomers, and is causing much discussion as to the probable effect on the earth should it pass through the comet's tail. Prof. Flammarion is of the opinion that the cyanogen gas would impregnate the atmosphere and possibly snuff out all life on the planet."

This, of course, was an astounding assertion. In retrospect and with the wisdom provided by seventy-six years of hindsight, it must be said, too, that it was almost as surprising that the editors of *The Times* placed it on page 1 of the newspaper. No wonder people were terrified four months hence when scientists and the press throughout the world were stating that the Earth would be literally engulfed in the comet's tail for four days in May.

Not that Camille Flammarion was a crackpot. He had been an astronomer at the prestigious Paris Observatory for several years, had been director of an observatory at Juvisy, outside Paris, had founded an astronomy journal, edited the *Bulletin of French Astronomical Studies*, and had to his credit as well a long list of publications. Among works often cited by other astronomers were his studies in the 1880s and 1890s of the surface of Mars, and his development of a theory that organic life on the Earth is modified by cyclical changes in the temperature of the Sun, that flowering chestnuts, lilacs, and the migratory habits of swallows, cuckoos, and nightingales, for instance, seem to be influenced to a marked degree by the fluctuations of solar activity. But Flammarion did seem to have somewhat of a penchant for doom; one of his books, in fact, was entitled *La Fin du Monde,* which he wrote in 1893 and which was what astronomers now regard as a highly sensationalized bit of speculation about how life on the Earth would end in collision with a comet. (Dr. Donald K. Yeomans at the Jet Propulsion Laboratory in Pasadena, California, has calculated that comets have struck the earth on the average of one every 33 million to 64 million years.) Moreover, although word of the new Yerkes discovery was said to have been communicated to many other astronomers as well, Flammarion was the only one who expressed the opinion that the cyanogen gas was going to impregnate the Earth's atmosphere and might destroy all life on the planet. There was no attempt in the news account to explain the basis for Flammarion's conclusions.

Indeed, the item went on to state that only once, as far as was known, had the Earth passed directly through the tail of Halley's Comet, and that no unusual physical occurrences on the Earth or in its atmosphere were associated with it other than meteor showers. Most astronomers did not agree with Flammarion, it was pointed out, "inasmuch as the tail of a comet is in a state of almost inconceivable rarefication, and believe that it would be repelled by the mass of the earth as it is by the light of the Sun. Also it is considered probable that the cyanogen of the comet's tail on contact with the earth's atmosphere would be decomposed by combustion into nitrogen and carbon dioxide, in quantities quite harmless to animal life."

Flammarion's name did not come up much more in the United States in connection with Halley's Comet, though he did later appear in the French press with his view altered to conform more to the notion that the cyanogen would be too diffuse to be dangerous. Nevertheless, the alarm his initial opinion conveyed never seemed to fade during the next four months as the comet circled the Sun, reached its closest approach to the Earth, and finally disappeared again. That was so even though *The Times* promptly followed the story with an editorial three days later attempting, despite its title, "Poison in the Tail of a Comet," to allay such fear. It read:

> People who were disturbed by the recent news that the "cyanogen line" had been found in the spectrum in the tail of Halley's comet by the astronomers at the Yerkes Observatory have now been kindly relieved of their anxiety by Prof. Hussey of the University of Michigan. He does not deny that cyanogen is a most terrible poison or that a comet would not have to add much of it to our atmosphere to destroy very promptly all terrestrial life. He only calls attention to the fact—which anybody, by the way, can find in any recent astronomical work—that the tails of comets are of such almost inconceivable tenuity, and that even though they were composed of nothing but cyanogen the earth could pass through a dozen of them without producing the slightest effect upon the most delicate of its inhabitants.
>
> Cometary tails are so near to nothing at all that the thinnest mist of which we have any knowledge is grossly material in comparison. The spectroscope's verdict is always beyond question, and wherever it finds cyanogen or anything else there the thing indicated by the "lines" undoubtedly exists, but the discovery, though sure, may mean amazingly little as to quantity, and such is undoubtedly the case in regard to comets. Only to ignorance or superstition are they alarming.

That is the generally accepted view among scientists today: Halley's Comet contains cyanogen, among other gases, of an incredibly small mass. Its particles are, in other words, spread so thin that cyanogen scarcely exists and thus poses no threat to man or planet passing through it.

As Halley's Comet reappeared from around behind the Sun in April 1910 and began its closest approach to the Earth, reports of its sightings came
thick and fast. By April 8, though it was still not
visible to the naked eye, astronomers peering
through the Lick telescope on Mount Hamilton at
about daylight spotted it, but only the head. The tail
was lost in the bright background of the rising Sun.
The comet was sighted as well the same night by
observers at Capetown, South Africa. On April 29
crewmen aboard a ship off Cape Hatteras sighted the
returning comet with magnified glasses and said it
was just barely visible with the naked eye. On that
same night, the Paris Astronomical Society announced that it was visible there, and a Rutgers professor saw it with the unaided eye at 2:30 in the
morning from his home in Highland Park, New
Jersey. It was due east slightly to the left of Venus,
he said, about four times as big as an ordinary star,
but not conspicuously bright.

It continued to grow brighter and larger, gradually
reaching the 1st magnitude, brighter than Polaris, or
the North Star, and its tail extended to what is believed to be a Halley's record—109 degrees, a distance that is 19 degrees more than halfway across
the sky.

Many people still alive as the comet was making
its 1986 reapproach saw it during that spring in
1910. One was Mrs. Earl Rahn of Whitesboro, New
York, who recalled that the comet looked to her like
a "peacock with a long beautiful tail. . . . And we
kids were scared because it was rumored that if the
tail touched the earth, it was the end of the world."
Another eyewitness, one eager to see the comet
again in his lifetime, was Oren A. Fellows of upper

(Opposite) As the comet made its nearest approach to Earth
in May 1910, it left an indelible impression on the viewers.
One called it a "peacock with a long beautiful tail. . . ." (The
Bettmann Archive)

New York State: "I was nine years old and someone had given me a small pair of binoculars. I was hooked. How well I remember the comet. It came in the northwest. At that time I was living in the country, and the view was impressive; bright, brilliant. I am now 82 years of age, not in too good health, but hope I am around to view it again."

Mrs. Rahn and Mr. Fellows wrote in one of several *Halley's Comet Watch Newsletters* published, in conjunction with the 1986 return, by Professor Joseph Laufter of Burlington County Community College in Pemberton, New Jersey. Several other vivid recollections were recorded as well.

> When I was 8, I woke one night to see the entire eastern sky lighted up. I went and woke my mother. We walked out to the end of the porch and watched it go across the sky. I've not ever seen such a beautiful display of nature. My mother told me what it was and she said I would probably live to see it again. I hope I can if my mind stays clear. The next morning I was telling about it at the breakfast table. My two brothers 10 and 12 said, "Why didn't you waken us?" Mother told them it would come every night for six or eight weeks. The next night she set the alarm and got us all up. . . . When I read of Christ's birth in the Bible and the great star that guided the shepherds, I think of Halley's.
>
> —Zoe Cooper, Cordell, Oklahoma

> As a 10 year old boy I watched Halley's. . . . It was very bright and the tail stretched half way across the sky.
>
> —Philip M. Beck, Beaver Falls, Pennsylvania

> . . . My interest is not for astronomical reasons but because there are well known and "accepted" predictions or prophecies concerning a comet which is given as encircling the earth for 4 days and causing horrendous damage and loss of life.
>
> —R.P.K., Bridgton, Maine

This was in the evening and still light enough to have taken pictures if we could have had a camera. . . . We were wondering if we would be killed if it hit the earth. Not only kids, but many older people. Hoping you can get a sight like we had without the fear that we had about being killed.

—Burney H. Moyer, Jonestown, Pennsylvania

I remember how they sold comet pills for when the earth passed through the comet's tail and comet insurance, and men of the cloth telling their congregation to bring all their money and valuables and storing them in the church. Then taking all and leaving town; and the suicides.

—Joseph Martin, Columbiana, Ohio

My parents said it was close to earth. Was large. Many people thought the world was going to end. Some were so scared they committed suicide.

—Mrs. M. Barron, Adrian, Michigan

The comet's appearance over the Ukraine is described by Frank Fershter, a Russian immigrant, in Dr. Jerred Metz's forthcoming book, *Halley's Comet, 1910: Days of Awe:*

It was a Sunday in 1910. An automobile passed by. It was the first time the people had ever seen an automobile. I had already seen one because I had been to different places. The peasants were smart people . . . but they weren't educated. They didn't know what to make of it. It was the time of Halley's comet. Some said it must be a part of Halley's comet. Someone said it must be something that brings the end of the world, and someone said a devil sits in there and operates the machine.

I don't know how the peasants knew about Halley's comet. The town where I lived, Bondorova, had about 15 blocks and I don't think among all of those people there were 10 that could read or write, but everybody knew that something was coming. I had a book that described Halley's comet. Somehow the peasants knew that I had it.

So they came up to me and said, "We want the
book that tells about the comet that will come
and destroy the earth." So I told them it's not as
bad as that. It won't destroy anything. I couldn't
tell them that nature provides the comet. If I told
them that, I'd have to explain all these things and I
didn't know anything about them myself. So I told
them it's God's doing and that's all. He'll see that
we're safe. . . . I remember just like today. There
was a bunch of Russian boys and girls visiting at
our house. That evening we were sitting around
the table and drinking tea and talking. One of the
fellows said goodnight. He was going home. All of
a sudden he comes back and he knocked at the
window. He said, "Come on out, ladies and gentlemen, and you'll see something."

We went outside and looked. . . . The comet was
almost as big as the moon. The comet and its tail
covered up almost the whole horizon. It made the
night like a street now looks when the street
lights are on. It was beautiful.

I still remember as I walked out of the house it
looked to me like the fiery tail was all on me. I
wasn't scared. I was stupefied. I didn't think of
God. I didn't think of nature. I thought just of that
thing. It looked like gold. The comet didn't have
any certain quality. It just looked like something
the imagination would make. It was a dream. It
was like being in space. It was such an experience.
I'll never forget it.


By May, the intensity of interest, fear, and excitement reached its climax. People began to fear that
the comet was going to collide with the Earth and
filled lecture halls where astronomers tried to assure
them that this could not happen; the closest it
would come, they said, would be 14 million miles
away. The closest it had ever come was in 837; the
distance then was 3 million miles.

King Edward VII died during the first week in
May, and a news service called United Wireless re-

ported that "queer things seemed to be going on around Halley's comet about the time of the accession of King George V."

In Bermuda on the night of Edward's death and the accession of his son, the news service said, the comet became visible and "a decidedly red tinge was noted in its tail."

> At 12:30 that night the fort at Hamilton, Bermuda, began to fire a salute of 101 guns in honor of the new King. An interval of two minutes elapsed between each discharge, and so the final gun was fired at 3:52 exactly.
>
> As the report died away, the observer saw a sudden flaring up at the end of the comet's tail. The head also glowed, a ball of red fire. For five minutes the phenomenon lasted, and was seen by the negroes at work on the docks. They were overcome with terror. They fell on their knees and began to pray. They thought that the end of the world was surely coming, and it was impossible to get them to go on with the loading of the Bermudian.
>
> Some of them connected the strange light with the death of King Edward. It showed, they declared, that war was sure to break out in King George's reign, and that some great calamity would befall the earth. They were speechless with fear and worked themselves up in their paroxysms of religious zeal to a perfect frenzy. It was not till the comet had faded from view and the daylight of Saturday had broken that they could be induced to go on again with their work.

Rumors abounded. A number of recent histories have recounted that an Oklahoma sheriff came to the aid of a local virgin who was being sacrificed to the comet: no authoritative source is given for the story, however, and indeed it seems to have no basis in fact. Others, in addition to Joseph Martin, tell of preachers or con men making off with money invested as a hedge against death. One Los Angeles real estate operator was said to have convinced a number of clients that the comet was, indeed, foretelling the end of the world. Halley's Comet was bearing down for a collision with the Earth of such force that the world would disappear. This agent did, however, have connections and could arrange to have half of his clients' money invested and set aside in Heaven. The Earth, of course, did not disappear, but he did— to Mexico with the money. And almost everywhere comet pills were being sold as antidotes to the approaching cyanogen gas.

In the major cities of the world comet parties were held nightly in crowded sidewalk cafés or on hotel roofs. Berliners climbed Kreuzberg Hill to watch. The Swiss climbed the Alps. A former All-American football player from Yale chartered a balloon to get a better view above Pittsfield, Massachusetts. On Friday the thirteenth, the Thirteen Club of New York assembled to counteract the effects of Halley's Comet; thirteen members sat at thirteen tables under thirteen umbrellas, and each member was instructed to spill salt on the table. The London *Daily Mail* reported an extraordinary amount of nervousness among "the lower class foreign population and the poorer Dutch and colored people are particularly anxious and seem to anticipate some disaster." In fact, it seemed often true that wherever there was undue concern, it was blamed on "foreigners," whether it be Johannesburg, the lower East Side of New York, or Wilkes-Barre, Pennsylvania. Miners in Wilkes-Barre, said to be chiefly "foreigners," refused to enter the anthracite mines. One is forced to wonder whether this wasn't a bit of xenophobia creeping through. One native New Yorker did complain in a letter to the editor of *The New York Times* that the women in his household were acting strangely, adding that he, "the only man about the house, had to combat a combination of tears, shudders and indifference" among the women. And, of course, back in Chicago, some of the native citizenry were upset as well. One disoriented man said the comet kept following him and colliding with him personally, and the city physician pronounced him insane. Two women, believing there to be no escape from the cyanogen, tried to end their own lives by turning on illuminating gas in their homes. One was rescued: the other was killed.

Monday May 16 began the four days of highest interest and concern. *The New York Times* page 1 lead story carried these headlines:

IN COMET'S TAIL
ON WEDNESDAY
European and American Astronomers Agree
the Earth Will
Not Suffer in the Passage
TELL THE TIMES ABOUT IT
And of Proposed Observations—Yerkes Observatory to Use Balloons if the Weather's Cloudy
TAIL 46,000,000 MILES LONG
Scarfed in a Filmy Bit of it, We'll Whirl On in Our
Dance Through Space, Unharmed, and, Most of
Us, Unheeding

An italic precede to the story stated that the general view of European and American astronomers and the general consensus was that, as the Earth passed through the tail of Halley's Comet, there would be no effect upon animal or vegetable life on Earth, perhaps no perceptible effect of any kind. But it was thought there might be meteoric and electrical manifestations in the atmosphere. It was estimated that the tail was 20 million to 40 million miles long, that if the Earth was going to pass through it, it would have to be only 15 million miles long. All agreed that the Earth was due to enter the

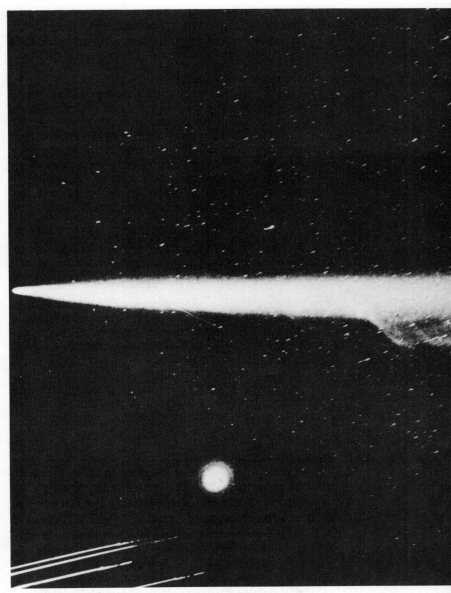

On May 13, 1910, the comet was photographed by a wide-angle camera at the Lowell Observatory, Flagstaff, Arizona. The streak across the comet near the coma is a meteor trail

and not a scratch on the negative. Streaks at the bottom are
the city lights of Flagstaff. The bright spot above the city
lights is Venus.

tail on Wednesday night at 11:20 P.M. and to emerge two hours later.

The story itself started as follows:

LONDON, May 15—Halley's comet, which has seemed the harbinger of so many misfortunes since 2616 B.C., the traditional year of Methusaleh's [sic] death, when, according to Sir Robert Hall, it visited terrestrial regions, reaches its climax of interest for this generation this week, in the course of which it crosses the sun's disk, makes its nearest approach to the earth, and rises first in the night sky.

It is now calculated that its nearest approach to the earth will be on Saturday, when it will be only 14,300,000 miles away, but before that, on Wednesday night, the comet will cross the sun's disk and the tail will stretch out in a straight line behind it, so that if its length is sufficient, we shall pass through it.

What will happen then, or whether anything will happen that will be perceptible to the ordinary man, are questions of daily debate. Among astronomers the general opinion is that even if the tail be sufficiently long to reach us, the world generally will be unaware that it is passing through the comet's tail. . . .

The long-awaited moment, 10:20 P.M. Wednesday night, May 18, 1910, arrived, the Earth apparently set to cut through a million miles of cyanogen gas. And what happened? Well, among other things, people in many parts of the world spent the next few hours in churches, offering continuous prayers. In San Juan, Puerto Rico, hundreds of people paraded in the streets, carrying candles and singing religious chants. Thousands of others lined Broadway. New York hotel roofs were a mob scene, as was Riverside Drive and as were the ferries and bridges on the rivers around Manhattan.

One observer in Westchester was excited to see

flashes illuminating the sky along the eastern horizon, but he became less so when he learned that he was watching beams from a Long Island Sound lighthouse. The 20,000 people on the Williamsburg Bridge were excited when some thought they saw the comet, with a reddish glow, so low in the western sky that it appeared to be rising right out of Manhattan. It was. What they were watching was a toy balloon with a red light attached. Several hundred men and women in spring furs or black tie thought they had heard the crack of doom and had seen the comet already upon them. What they saw and heard instead was the crack of a 1910 photographer's flash-powder.

In short, no one seemed to have died from the comet's fumes. Moreover, no one seemed even to have seen it. New Yorkers noticed no effects at all, ill or otherwise, and by midnight the crowds had begun to dwindle. Harold Jacoby, an astronomy professor at Columbia University, who stationed himself on Riverside Drive from 10:30 P.M. until midnight, concluded then that "the fact that the comet's tail has not been visible at the time of its contact with the earth, which must now be chiefly past, is a vindication for the general belief of astronomers that the tail is so thin that its presence near us is undetectable."

But the diehards were still watching. At 1 A.M., Prof. E. B. Frost of the Yerkes Observatory on Williams Bay in Wisconsin said: "We have passed through the comet's tail, and we are no wiser than we were before."

Then at 2 A.M., just after the Moon had set, a group of observers in the tower on top of *The New York Times* spotted a band of light 100 degrees in length stretching from the eastern horizon over the Queensboro Bridge. Mary Proctor, an astronomer hired by *The Times* to cover the comet, identified it as the outer boundary of the comet's tail, extending

up through the square of Pegasus and Aquarius to
Aquila. At its widest part, just beneath the first magnitude star Altair, the width of the band was about
ten degrees, and throughout its length it had a
brightness equal to that of the Milky Way.

The next day astronomers around the world confirmed Mary Proctor's report. Describing his own
sighting, Professor Frost said later that at about two
o'clock on the morning of May 19, the

> never-to-be forgotten spectacle was presented of
> the comet so near at hand as to extend over one
> hundred degrees from beyond the meridian far
> down to the eastern horizon, like the white beam
> of a powerful searchlight. It equaled in brightness
> the light of the Milky Way, and was not less than
> five degrees broad at the horizon, below which lay
> the head, to be lost in the glare of dawn when it
> did rise some time later. Faint and less definitely
> marked, this was seen in nearly the same place in
> the sky on the three following mornings, as is now
> known from reports from stations favored with
> fair weather. . . .

But there was definitely a hitch: The notorious
tail of Halley's Comet was in the wrong place. It was
in the east, when most astronomers had predicted
its appearance in the west. If that was truly the case,
did the Earth, as expected, pass through the cyan-
ogenous tail at some point during the preceding
hours? Moreover, the comet seemed somehow lost.
After some 2,000 years of impeccable navigation,
had it strayed badly off course, or had the astronomers been wrong? One theory was that the comet
had simply dropped its tail, which was then drifting
off to regions unknown.

On Friday, May 20, the headline of the lead story
on page 1 of *The Times* read:

DIDN'T GET THROUGH THE COMET'S TAIL

Professor Jacoby, professing admiration for the patience and perseverance of Miss Proctor for staying up, spotting, and reporting the comet's appearance in the east, said he was never more surprised than when he read in *The Times* that morning that the Earth had evidently not been through the comet's tail at all.

Professor Frost, describing his observances Thursday, said that after the tail appeared in the eastern sky, it then mysteriously appeared in the west at the same time. It was in the east, he said, "even after the head of the comet had been observed in the western sky after sunset and with a tail of considerable length. At noon, a particularly beautiful display of iridescent clouds, which may be untechnically called a horizontal rainbow, was observed." Mary Proctor professed to have the answers. She wrote that the seeming anomaly, of the tail appearing to be in both the east and the west, did not necessarily mean that astronomers had miscalculated:

> It would now appear that at least a portion of the tail swept by the earth on the morning of the 19th, and that we were within the forks of separate streamers of it for the days following, so that necessarily one portion of the tail would be to the east and the other to the west. . . . Undoubtedly, we passed through the train of the comet about noon on May 19, and the rainbow effect was probably caused by cometary particles glistening in the glare of sunlight.

She was not right, as discoveries in the 1950s would make clear. But she was not far off. Through the use of advanced spectroscopy, scientists have determined that the comet often has two tails, not one: (1) an extended ion, or plasma, tail, which is a mélange of many gases, is antisolar in direction—that is, because of solar winds, it always stretches away from the Sun, regardless of whether the comet itself is traveling toward the Sun or away from it; (2) the other tail is composed of dust from the interior of the comet and curves out essentially in a direction and in a form that looks something like a stream from a rotating lawn sprinkler.

Thanks to those discoveries and thanks to the development of high-speed computers, astronomers in the 1980s have a much clearer "view" of what went on during that famous night of May 18, 1910, than Mary Proctor did from *The Times* tower, or than Professor Jacoby did from Riverside Drive or E. B. Frost from Williams Bay, Wisconsin. In the spring of 1984, at the request of the science department of *The Times*, Dr. Donald K. Yeomans dug up the coordinates reported by various 1910 astronomers. He fed them into his computer at the Jet Propulsion Laboratory at Pasadena. Yes, he said, the Earth was swept by the tail of Halley's Comet in 1910—by both tails, one appearing in the east and one in the west.

The current sighting of Halley's Comet ushers in a time when some of the most remarkable discoveries ever imagined about the universe can be made from orbiting Earth observatories using wavelengths in the electromagnetic spectrum invisible to the human eye. Halley's Comet—once again, the signal for a new era of astronomy.

# FIVE

# Comets—
# The Mystery,
# the Science

**Where Do** One of the endearing qualities of Halley's Comet is
**Comets** that it embodies a number of certainties. It regularly
**Come From?** swings in from the outer limits of its orbit, beyond
Neptune, to circle the Sun closer than the Earth does
in its orbit—but not as close as the planet Mercury
—and then it heads out again.

A full three years before the comet would make
anything like a close approach to Earth, astronomers
were already aiming their probing instruments into
the depths of the planetary system to get the first
glimpse of the comet doing what it was bound to do:
make its way back toward the brilliance of the Sun.

The expectation was that it would begin to glow
far from the Sun, glow energetically enough to be
seen. And there was high confidence in the calculations that predicted its path. In October 1982, the
200-inch Mount Palomar telescope, the world's second largest, was able to claim a kind of victory. It
was the first to spot the returning comet, photo-
graphing it as a faint, starlike object. The powerful
Palomar saw it farther out than it had ever been seen
before, 11 astronomical units (each unit is the mean
distance from Earth to Sun, 93 million miles). Soon

thereafter it was also observed by very large telescopes at La Silla in Chile, atop Kitt Peak in Arizona,
and Mauna Kea in Hawaii.

The fact that Halley's is so reassuringly regular
that in its travels its image can be plucked from the
sky at a great distance belies the mysteries that still
surround the paths of comets in general.

For one thing, where do they come from? There
must be new comets coursing into the planetary system all the time. Recent evidence makes that clear.

When IRAS, the Infrared Astronomical Satellite
launched early in 1983, detected five new comets
that had not been observed from Earth before, it
spotted them at an average rate of almost once a
month. According to Rüdeger Reinhard, leader of
the European Space Agency's mission to Halley,
about 100 new comets probably enter the inner Solar
System each year. Many are thrown out again but a
few have been diverted into short-period orbits that
do not carry them much farther from the Sun than
Jupiter and skirt so close to the Sun that they are
unlikely to survive more than a few hundred orbits
before they are burned away.

While passing through the inner part of the Solar
System, the comets, heated by sunlight, give off dust
and gas to form misty envelopes, or comas, and, buf-
feted by the solar wind, this material is dragged
away to form tails. Sometimes, comets split into
pieces, each of the pieces like the others, traveling
together like a string of migrating ducks.

Those comets that skirt the Sun at close range
may never reappear at all. A telescope riding the Defense Department satellite P78-1 has inadvertently
recorded the disappearance of at least three Sun-
grazing comets. The device is a Naval Research Laboratory coronagraph designed to view the corona, or
glowing halo, around the Sun normally seen only
during an eclipse. In a coronagraph the brilliant solar
image is artificially eclipsed. The goal of the Navy

New comets seem to be cruising into the planetary system all the time. In 1983, the Infrared Astronomical Satellite detected five new comets never observed from Earth before. (*NASA*)

experiment was to monitor activity in the corona and explore its links to events on the Sun and the solar wind. Examination of its recordings, after they were received on Earth, revealed the images of three comets flying toward the Sun on August 30, 1979, January 26, 1981, and July 20, 1981. Subsequent calculation of their trajectories by Brian Marsden of the Smithsonian Astrophysical Observatory indicated that they were destined to pass closer to the center of the Sun than the Sun's own radius. Thus they were destined to plunge into the solar surface, but must have been vaporized by intense heat before doing so. Such observations could never have been

made from Earth because scattered sunlight makes
the daytime sky far too bright. The chance observation of these three comet deaths indicates that many
more comets die each year than was previously supposed.

At first, it might seem that Halley's is headed for
an early demise, too. A comet like Halley's, which is
at most a few miles in diameter, can shed a tail 100
million miles long as well as a coma, or dust-gas envelope, 100,000 miles wide. It is, in effect, leaving
itself behind. But the amount of cometary material
shed is not really very large. And the tail is utterly
diaphanous. So insubstantial is the material of a
comet tail that stars shine through it with no evident loss of brightness. The tail is only visible at all
because the tiny dust particles in it are such mar-
velous reflectors of sunlight. In the tail their reflective efficiency is 100 million times greater than
when the material was consolidated. The same kind
of phenomenon can be seen in everyday life when
motes—the tiniest particles of dust and bits of other
things that ought to be invisible—can be seen adrift
in a sunbeam.

Thus despite its grand tail, scientists estimate
that on each circuit of the Sun, Halley's Comet
sheds only 1 millionth of its material. Since these
passages are spaced about seventy-six years apart, it
will obviously take a long time for the comet to
wither away. But some day it will, and so will all the
other comets hazarding repeated passage around the
Sun. And the comets that die will be replaced. The
astonishing fact is that the Solar System is continually leaking comets into space. And this presumably
has been going on ever since the Solar System was
formed, some 4.6 billion years ago. What accounts
for it? Is there a comet factory out there somewhere?

Until 1577 Europeans assumed comets—as well
as fireballs and meteors—were somehow formed
within the atmosphere. There were some similari-

ties among these objects and thus they were all joined together in one theory. But obviously a comet was not a meteor. Fireballs and meteors (or "shooting stars") streak across the sky at fiery speeds. A comet seems to move so slowly that only on a succession of nights does its position among the stars change substantially. The tail gives an impression of great velocity, but that is deceptive, for when a comet is moving away from the Sun its tail reaches out in front of it. The tail is not left behind, like the condensation trail behind a jet. It is swept away from the comet by sunlight and by a "wind" blowing out from the Sun. Hence the tail can even precede the comet much as smoke is blown ahead of a ship steaming downwind.

It took the great Tycho Brahe, the Danish astronomer who produced meticulous astronomical observations that would confirm that Earth and other planets orbit the Sun, to discern that comets came from somewhere far from the Earth's atmosphere.

Toward the end of the eighteenth century Pierre Simon, Marquis de Laplace, took a position at the other extreme from the one that asserted comets were formed near Earth. He proposed that comets were brief visitors from far out in space. But if that were the case they would plunge into the Solar System at extremely high velocity, so fast in fact that they would circle the Sun, and then fly away forever. By today's reasoning, he was wrong, at least in part. Most comets seem to come from the outer part of the Solar System. The marquis may have had a point, though. Otto Struve, first head of the National Radio Astronomy Observatory in West Virginia, pointed out much later that the fact that comets from distant space have not been seen plunging into the Solar System does not mean they never do so. It is probable that only a tiny percentage of the comets that enter the inner Solar System are ever observed. Indeed, our view of the comets is ex-

**Simon, marquis de Laplace.**

tremely biased, since only those that come close
enough to the Sun to become luminous are seen, and
by then the orbits of virtually all of them have been
altered by the planets.

In another way the marquis had a point, too. Even
though comets generally are believed to originate
somewhere in the Solar System, many of them nevertheless manage to circle the Sun, then fly out
into space and disappear. This has less to do with
their speed, however, than it does with the paths
they take (and their disappearance is not as mysterious as it sounds in that their orbits have usually
been well calculated).

If a comet is part of the Solar System, one would
expect it to remain within that system indefinitely
—that is, in closed orbit around the Sun. Yet, some
comets journey along open orbits that allow them to
escape the Solar System and join the stars. Evidently, their orbits were not always open and were
altered in some way, perhaps by the pull of planets.

To see how a comet might take a route that allows it to escape the pull of the Sun, it is important to look closely at the various possible paths they can take. A free-flying body under the sole gravitational control of the Sun will follow one of four paths, known as conic sections because they are usually displayed by slicing through a cone at different angles. If one cuts across the cone at right angles to its central axis the resulting curve is a circle. An ellipse is produced if one slices a cone diagonally so as to cut both of its sloping sides. That is the path flown by all objects in closed orbits, although the planets orbit the Sun in ellipses that are almost circular. A slice parallel to the outer slope of a cone forms a parabola. Other slices that do not cut both slopes produce hyperbolas. Since neither parabolas nor hyperbolas form a closed figure, comets traveling either kind of path may never return. Only comets in elliptical paths—like Halley's—can be counted on to reappear again and again.

As of 1978 hundreds of individual comets had been tracked, a number of them on more than one return visit. They were tracked with sufficient accuracy to determine the precise nature of their orbits. Bertram Donn and Jurgen Rahe of NASA's Goddard Space Flight Center, reporting on 658 orbits, said 42

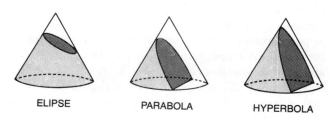

ELIPSE            PARABOLA            HYPERBOLA

A free-flying object under gravitational control of the Sun will follow paths known as "conic sections."

percent of the orbits were elliptical, 43 percent were
slightly parabolic and 15 percent were moderately
hyperbolic. (None were in the wide hyperbolas expected of a visitor from distant space.) Why were so
many in open orbits? In 1927 the Belgian-born astronomer, G. Van Biesbroeck, did a detailed compu-
tation of the orbit of Comet Delavan, whose path
through the inner Solar System had clearly been hyperbolic. By retracing its inbound route among the
planets and allowing for their gravitational effects,
he found that its earlier orbit had been an extremely
narrow ellipse, reaching out 170,000 astronomical
units, which carried it one third of the way to the
nearest star. To complete one trip around that orbit
took 24 million years. Another of his analyses
showed that Comet Morehouse, first sighted in
1908, flew a 500,000-year orbit. The conviction grew
that the orbits of all known comets were probably
elliptical to begin with but that many were altered
by passage among the planets.

## The Great Oort Cloud

At the moment the most popular concept concerning the source of comet renewals is one that grew
out of a 1932 proposal by the Estonian astronomer
Ernst Öpik, later elaborated by Jan Oort, a lean and
courtly Dutchman. At Oort's disposal in 1950 were
a number of highly elongated comet orbits determined by Van Biesbroeck and others. There was a
strong tendency for the outermost reach of these orbits to lie in a vast spherical region between 30,000
and 100,000 astronomical units in all directions
from the Sun. This was far beyond the outer planets
and almost halfway to the nearest stars, but still
within the gravitational grip of the Sun.

Oort therefore proposed that this vast spherical region is the home of a great cloud of comets moving
at little more than a walking pace and requiring mil-

Jan Oort.

lions of years for one circuit of the Sun. To have provided a reservoir sufficiently large to keep supplying the comets that, after billions of years, are still penetrating to visible range, the comets in Oort's Cloud would have to number in the hundreds of billions. The orbits of these comets are thought to be tilted at all angles to the ecliptic (the orbits of the planets), forming—in the words of Thomas Gold of Cornell University—a pattern "like a ball of yarn."

Oort suggested that early in the history of the Solar System a planet orbiting the Sun between Mars and Jupiter exploded. If it were like Jupiter, such a planet could have contained enough lightweight material to produce billions of comets, which were widely thought to have rocky cores. Some of the heavier material, Oort said, survives as the asteroids and meteorites that still clutter the region between Mars and Jupiter, but most of the debris was scattered by crack-the-whip effects from the gravity of surviving planets, notably Jupiter. Oort envisioned that this process scattered the explosion debris in all directions. Some flew off into space, ended up in the Sun, or fell onto the planets, but hundreds of billions of the lighter fragments remained in orbit far beyond the outermost planets, forming the so-called Oort Cloud.

In 1978 Thomas C. Van Flandern of the celestial mechanics branch of the United States Naval Observatory in Washington proposed that the planetary explosion occurred only a few million years ago. But while the concept of the Oort Cloud is now generally accepted, Oort's exploding-planet hypothesis for the cloud's creation has now been rejected by many astronomers, in part because the estimated combined mass of all asteroids and meteorites does not approach that of any existing planet. Nevertheless, some supporters of the idea hold it open as a possibility, noting that 97 percent of the exploded material was probably thrown out of the Solar System.

Only a small percentage would have ended up in the
Oort Cloud and asteroid belt.

One reason to believe in the cloud's existence is
that so many of the "new" comets making their first
entry into the inner Solar System seem in orbits
whose outer limits lie in the region described by
Oort, between 30,000 and 100,000 astronomical
units from the Sun. These new comets, like those
that are in orbits that only rarely bring them close to
the Sun, such as Halley's, tend to be the brightest.
(The Jovian comets are often observed only through
telescopes, having been so depleted by passages of
the Sun that they are rarely bright enough for naked-
eye observation.)

If one accepts the notion of the Oort Cloud, that
acceptance leads to some wonderful speculation. For
instance, it may be that all stars have clouds of comets like the Oort Cloud, and the clouds are, cosmic-
ally speaking, near each other. The Oort Cloud is
believed to lie about halfway to the nearest star,
Proxima Centauri, some 270,000 astronomical units
away. Hence, the comet cloud of this Solar System
may be rubbing elbows with comet clouds of our
neighbors, and the clouds may sometimes exchange
comets. If other planetary systems like our own
have also been ejecting comets, space between the
stars may be a sea of wandering comets.

In 1968 the Czech-born comet specialist Zdenek
Sekanina proposed that in the great void between
stars there are a thousand billion comets per cubic
parsec. This is not a very great density since one parsec is the distance traveled by light in 3.26 years.
Nevertheless, Sekanina suggested that the Oort
Cloud is sometimes enriched by capturing such
comets. That is because the cloud itself is pictured
as so vast. It is possible that it could contain all the
comets astronomers say it does, and those comets
would still be less close together than the occasional
cometary voyagers spotted toward the heart of the
Solar System.

One of the more intriguing propositions concerning this Oort Cloud is that it is sometimes penetrated by stars, all of which are on the move relative to one another, which would scatter comets in all directions. In 1954 Soviet astronomers calculated that, since the formation of Earth and other planets some 4.6 billion years ago, 3,000 stars have passed through the heart of the Oort Cloud. Giving support to this idea, at least until recently, was the belief that new comets tended to arrive in groups, implying that each group was the product of a specific stellar intrusion. By 1982, however, statistical analyses of all available records by Fred Whipple, Lubor Kresák of Czechoslovakia, and others indicated that there was, in fact, no significant grouping.

Assuming for a moment that the Oort Cloud does exist, there is a stunning sidelight that ought to be mentioned. It is a sidelight, anyway, insofar as the universe is concerned, but of vital importance to the inhabitants of Earth. The cloud has recently been implicated in the mass extinctions that sometimes devastate this planet.

Fred Whipple.

To account for the disappearance of the dinosaurs and the other great extinctions, it was proposed in 1984 that the Oort Cloud is penetrated on a regular basis by a particular nearby star that was given the name Nemesis and, with macabre humor, dubbed the death star in press reports. The star, according to this thinking, scatters part of the cloud, showering the inner Solar System with a million or more comets, some of which bombard the Moon and planets, including Earth, bringing destruction to many forms of life.

It was not entirely a new idea, this notion that comets sometimes play the role of villain on Earth. In the 1960s Harold C. Urey, who won a Nobel Prize in 1934 for his discovery of heavy water (deuterium oxide), proposed that each geologic period was terminated by the impact of a comet, causing widespread extinctions.

In 1979 two astronomers at the Royal Observatory in Edinburgh, W. M. Napier and S. V. M. Cube, argued that such bombardments occur when the Solar System passes through one of the spiral arms of the Milky Way Galaxy, crowded with stars, dust clouds —and perhaps asteroids, meteorites, and comets. The Sun and its family of planets are circling in a gigantic system of spiral star clouds whose nearest portions are seen as the Milky Way. The spiral structure is not directly visible, since we are embedded within it, but we can look out through our galaxy and see others whose spiral structure resembles that of storm clouds in a hurricane viewed from space. Napier and Cube argued that the Sun and planets pass through a spiral arm every few tens of millions of years, and during such passages the Solar System picks up a new population of asteroids, meteorites, and comets. Such encounters, they said, accounted for mass extinctions, ice ages, widespread cratering of the inner planets, and gouging out of the landscape on arid Mars by water of cometary origin. The last passage through a spiral arm occurred less than 10 million years ago, they said.

Dr. Harold C. Urey.

The idea that the great extinctions might have been caused by impacts of comets or asteroids became far more plausible with the 1978 discovery of a thin layer of strongly enriched iridium in sediments apparently laid down at the time when the dinosaurs became extinct. That element is scarce in surface rocks of Earth but relatively abundant in meteorites. The 1968 Nobel laureate Luis W. Alvarez, his son Walter, and two other colleagues at the University of California in Berkeley reported in 1980 that this telltale iridium layer had been found in Italy, Denmark, and New Zealand. Similar reports soon came from other sites. Then, in 1981, Jack Hills of the Los Alamos National Laboratory in New Mexico joined what he called the me-too parade, proposing that penetration by a passing star of a comet belt between

Dr. Luis W. Alvarez.

the Oort Cloud and outer planets could send a lethal shower of comets toward the Earth.

In 1984, David M. Raup and J. John Sepkoski, Jr., of the University of Chicago reported that over the past 250 million years mass extinctions, in some of which 90 percent of marine species vanished, have tended to occur about every 30 million years. Michael R. Rampino and Richard B. Stothers of NASA's Institute for Space Studies in New York City found that this was approximately the occurrence rate of impacts that have left identifiable craters on the earth. They suggested that the Solar System, at intervals of about 33 million years, crosses the central plane of the galaxy, thereby becoming exposed to unusually severe bombardment. Finally the Berkeley group proposed that the Sun is actually in a two-star system, its companion being a small, faint star that they named Nemesis. At intervals of roughly 28 million years, they said, its orbit brings it close enough to penetrate the Oort Cloud and send a deluge of a million comets into the inner Solar System. At least one, they said, would hit the Earth with enough energy to cause a catastrophic explosion. If that happened on land, it would load the high atmosphere, or stratosphere, with sufficient dust particles to cut off sunlight and chill the climate, killing off many species. A similar effect has been proposed as a by-product of nuclear war—a so-called nuclear winter that would annihilate a large part of humanity and render many species extinct.

But that is only one view. It is not truly clear just how devastating a comet impact would be. It is not, in fact, even certain that most comet heads could survive their fiery passage through the atmosphere. The manner in which some comets break up during unimpeded flight through space suggests that their cores are not very cohesive.

Nevertheless, George W. Wetherill of the Carnegie Institution of Washington, an authority on meteorites, fireballs, and the like, suspects that a plunging comet head 1 mile in diameter would carry so much punch that it "would not see the atmosphere" and slice right through it. It would strike the Earth sufficiently intact to explode with great violence. At least one or two scientists even believe such an object would penetrate the ocean and blast part of the sea floor into the sky.

There is indeed evidence of an explosion in 1908 that may have been cometary. In that year, a comet fragment less than 200 feet in diameter may have plunged into the atmosphere over Siberia. The result was the Tunguska explosion, which in many ways was like a high-altitude hydrogen bomb explosion, and its cause—whether it was a comet or something else entirely—has been debated long and hard for years.

Trees were felled within a radius of many miles, and the forest was set ablaze. Horses were knocked off their feet more than 100 miles away. Atmospheric shock waves circled the earth. Many reindeer were killed, but fortunately no humans seem to have been close enough for severe injury. The explosion occurred so high in the atmosphere that no crater was formed on the Earth's surface. Many explanations have been advanced, such as the explosion of a spaceship from another world, a meteorite made of antimatter, or a black hole. Lubor Kresák of Czechoslovakia, however, pointed out that the event coincided with one of the annual Taurid meteor showers. These showers, during which "shooting stars" may be visible more than once a minute, occur as the Earth, in its orbital flight around the Sun, passes through the orbit of a comet that has been shedding material. This particular shower takes place as the Earth crosses the orbit of Comet Encke—the one with the shortest period of reappearance known, circling the Sun every 3.3 years. Kresák suggested that the Tunguska explosion was produced by a large chunk that had been shed by

Encke but was still following its orbital racetrack. Skeptics have questioned why the comet was not seen approaching. One proposed explanation was that it was no longer luminous—a former "dirty snowball" whose frozen gas had all been dissipated, after repeated passages of the Sun, leaving only a dark residue.

**The Birth of Comets**  When Comet Halley loops into view, some people will stare up there to see the splendor of it. And that will suffice. Others will look up in the hope of learning some truths about the nature of comets. And that will make them happy. But some will look up at that radiant celestial body and see so far beyond it into the past that they will be observing a piece of the birth of the Solar System. Comets, it seems, are no mere flashes in the heavens but an integral part of them. So, while it is one thing to wonder where these visitors come from now—probably that aggregation of comets surrounding the Solar System called the Oort Cloud—it is another, almost mystical question to ask: Where do Halley and all those others *really* come from, all the way back there in the earliest of stirrings, in the primordial gases?

Although comets often come as close to Earth as any celestial body except the Moon, astronomers remain mystified as to how they came into being. While there are records of roughly 1,300 individual comets, only about thirty have been observed at positions beyond the orbit of Jupiter and, at last report, only six at the distance of Saturn or beyond. Since there is no evidence that any substantial number come from outer space, there must be a closer source, some theorists believed. And this led to the revival of a proposition advanced in the eighteenth century by the French mathematician Joseph Louis, Comte Lagrange. Perhaps, he said, the comets were blown out of the giant planets, which were then as-

sumed to be hot bodies like the Sun, rather than the
frigid bodies we now know them to be. The composition of comets seems strikingly like that of the
planets Neptune and Uranus. This, it was thought,
could mean either that the comets come out of such
planets or that the reverse was true, with the planets
originally assembled from cometary material. As
more and more comet orbits were calculated, the
idea that at least some comets originate in Jupiter
became more plausible since the aphelia of so many
of them—the points in their orbits farthest from the
Sun—were near the orbit of Jupiter. At last count
this was true of about 100, now known because of
their seeming link to Jupiter as the Jovian comets.

The nineteenth-century proposal, as recounted by
the British astronomer Patrick Moore, envisioned
the great red spot on Jupiter as "a kind of supervol-
cano, puffing out comets regularly." The great red
spot is a semipermanent, swirling feature within the
turbulent Jovian clouds.

Another feature linking the Jovian comets with
that planet is the similarity of their orbital planes.
Unlike many comets, the planets all orbit the Sun
close to a common plane, like coins scattered on a
table top. That plane, known as the ecliptic, is de-
fined by the orbit of the Earth extended out into the
heavens. If we could see the stars in daytime, the
Sun would appear to follow the ecliptic as the Earth
moves around it. The apparent paths of the planets
lie close to the same plane. On the other hand, the
orbits of long-period comets—those that, like Halley's, range far out from the Sun—are tilted at many
angles to the ecliptic. Those of the Jovian group,
however, lie relatively close to the ecliptic and,
therefore, to the plane of Jupiter's own orbit. Furthermore, most of them circle the Sun in the same
direction as that planet. While some astronomers
see this as evidence that the comets originated in
Jupiter, the conventional explanation is that they

were originally long-period comets but were yanked or repeatedly nudged by Jupiter's gravity into orbits that no longer carry them much farther out than Jupiter itself.

A remarkable finding, reported in 1981 by A. Carusi and G. B. Valsecchi based on their analysis of the orbital histories of twenty-two short-period comets, was that during the past two centuries seven of them had become short-lived satellites of Jupiter. One, Comet P/Gehrels 3, was captured three times, in one case for seven years. As planners of manned missions to the Moon knew very well, a passing spacecraft does not readily go into orbit around such a body. It must be carefully nudged by rocket thrust. Otherwise it either crashes into the body or sails past it. The comets captured by Jupiter may have been nudged by gas blowing off their own surfaces, been slowed by passage through the upper Jovian atmosphere, or, most likely, by close encounters with something orbiting Jupiter.

The proposal of a Jovian origin of comets has met with widespread doubt for a number of reasons. One has to do with Jupiter's impressive size. Jupiter, by far the largest of the planets, has a powerful gravity field. It is almost as massive as a star. Most stars, apart from our own, are in two-star or three-star groupings, and some astronomers therefore regard Jupiter as "a star that failed," the solar sibling that never developed. It never grew quite big enough to create the pressure and temperature in its core needed to ignite the nuclear fires that make stars shine. Because of Jupiter's enormous mass, a comet, to escape from it, would have to be expelled at 37 miles per second, compared to an escape velocity of only 7 miles per second for Earth.

The chief modern proponent of the idea that Jupiter periodically gives birth to comets has been S. K. Vsekhsviatsky at the Kiev Observatory in the Soviet Union. His initial proposal in 1953 evoked little enthusiasm, particularly since it was then known that, far from being volcanic, the planet is at least partly frigid and covered with swirling clouds. Vsekhsviatsky then proposed that comets are thrown out from Jupiter's four inner moons—known as the Galilean moons because they were large and bright enough to have been discovered by Galileo. While only a limited number of comets are in orbits linked to Jupiter, Vsekhsviatsky argued that the giant planet's gravity could throw a comet into virtually any orbit, large or small, if the comet passed Jupiter in the right manner.

This is a trick that has been used by planners of space missions to alter a spacecraft's trajectory and send it hurtling toward new targets (and, in some cases, entirely out of the Solar System). If the craft passes behind Jupiter in the planet's orbital flight around the Sun, Jovian gravity gives the spacecraft a tremendous yank. A tiny fraction of the planet's orbital momentum is transferred to the spacecraft. The effect on mighty Jupiter is utterly insignificant, but its influence on the spacecraft is spectacular. The difficulty with this explanation of diverse comet orbits, however, is that Jupiter is so efficient a pitcher of comets that most would be thrown either into infinite space or into the Sun, requiring a high rate of local comet production to account for the number observed.

Proponents of a Jovian explanation might take heart from evidence of eruptions on at least one Jovian moon, gathered by the spacecraft Voyager 1, which flew close to Io, Jupiter's inner moon, in 1979. It recorded what appeared to be a volcanic eruption on Io's horizon, and the surface of that moon showed signs of widespread volcanism, attributed to the great tidal stresses induced in Io's interior by its proximity to Jupiter. Nevertheless, few astronomers regard eruptions on Jovian moons as a likely source of comets.

The most widely publicized proposition regarding Jupiter as a source of comets was that in Immanuel Velikovsky's best-selling book *Worlds in Collision* published in 1950. He said Venus was born as a comet ejected by Jupiter and originally had a tail of poisonous material that swept past the Earth during the period when Egypt was beset by the biblical plagues, darkening the sky with a "tempest of cinders." Astronomers scoffed at the idea on numerous grounds. Venus is now in a stable, almost circular orbit occupying the slot between the orbits of Mercury and Earth, where a planet should have formed according to the accepted hypothesis for evolution of the Solar System. Furthermore, the masses of the largest comet heads ever observed resemble those of hills or mountains, rather than planets the size of Earth and Venus.

*Broader, More Plausible Theories*

Plausible theories about cometary evolution abound. It is possible—and the arguments along these lines are persuasive—that comets are like the distant planets, made of the same stuff, but they simply never joined together to become a larger body. And it is thus reasonable to look up into the sky as Halley journeys by and see a piece of the early Solar System, trapped in a great orbit around the Sun, that could just as well have had a very different existence, merging into Jupiter or becoming a small piece of Neptune. To use a marine analogy, it is as if Halley's Comet were a single organism such as a sponge or a coral that had never found its way to the larger colony and thus—tiny but still a complete being—it floats on and on in the celestial sea.

Since the history of comets and that of the entire Solar System seem intertwined, the question of cometary origins can perhaps best be answered in terms of the formation of the whole system. For a long time it was widely believed that the planets and

other bodies orbiting the Sun were formed when another star came by at close range. The gravity of each
star pulled material out of the other one to form the
inner and outer planets. But that concept has been
discarded in favor of one resembling that proposed
more than 300 years ago by René Descartes and similar to one put forward by Immanuel Kant later. The
Sun and its companions, it was said, evolved from a
swirling cloud of material. After many modifica-
tions and challenges by alternate concepts, this hypothesis remains a widely accepted view. However,
there is almost nothing about the formation of the
Solar System on which all astronomers will agree.
This theory is far from complete and full of inconsis-
tencies.

The present concept is based on what astronomers
now see elsewhere in nearby parts of the Milky Way
Galaxy: a giant, gently turbulent cloud of dust, gas,
and molecules (that, from their radio emissions, are
of extremely diverse chemical composition) laden
with enough material to make scores of stars and
planetary families. Harvard's Fred Whipple cites the
Trifid Nebula as a good example.

This view of a system's formation holds that, at
first, the cloud is composed of regions rotating gently in random directions, but as they collide repeatedly they begin to sort themselves out into cells of
predominant rotation. One of these cells is the
cloud, or nebula, destined to be drawn together gravitationally to become the Solar System. Which is
fine as far as it goes. But a question often raised is
this: As long as the cloud's dust, gas, and diverse
molecules is widely dispersed, where is the concen-
tration of material—the "center of gravity"—sufficiently dense to begin pulling the material together?
The answer, many astronomers believe, is that one
or more shock waves from nearby stellar explosions,
or supernovas, might pass through the cloud, pro-

ducing concentrations of material sufficient to initiate gravitational collapse around many centers.

The concept has been buttressed as our view of the heavens has sharpened through improved observing techniques. It has become evident that supernova shock waves are radiating outward from numerous centers, pushing luminous veils of gas in front of them. Some celestial photographs resemble a great bubble bath of such supernova remnants. If that kind of observation makes this theory plausible, another piece of evidence makes it even more so. It appears to be the case that the supernova occurred just at the same time it would have been needed to start the birth of the Solar System. Scientists came to that conclusion with the discovery in some meteorites of what appears to be debris from one or more such events.

It was about 4.6 billion years ago that the part of the nebula destined to form the Solar System began concentrating itself around one center of attraction. Hundreds of other stars may also have been forming nearby in the same manner. From what we see in other clouds where new stars appear to be forming, it seems likely that roughly 100 stars grew out of the original supercloud. In an analysis of ways in which the comets might have come into being, Jack Gilbert Hills of the Los Alamos National Laboratory has proposed that some stellar neighbors of the evolving Sun may have been considerably less distant than the Oort Cloud of today. The night sky of that era—had there been a planet and people on it to look upward—would have looked very different from that of today, decked with glowing nebulae and nearby protostars. Ultimately, however, the stars shed mass, weakening their gravitational attraction for their neighbors, and were dispersed to considerably greater distances.

As the Sun's own nebula shrank to smaller size,

its rotation rate increased to conserve its angular (or rotational) momentum and the shrinking nebula condensed from a sphere into a flattened disk. Until one pattern of rotation became universal, the collapsing cloud was stirred into violent turbulence. In Whipple's view, the bulk of the material initially became concentrated into two spheres, and in one of those spheres the central pressure and temperature were sufficiently high to initiate the fusion of hydrogen atoms into helium—the reaction that makes the Sun shine. The other sphere—the planet Jupiter— failed to acquire enough mass to become a star, although its core is very hot and the planet gives off slightly more heat than it gains from sunlight. Unlike the other planets, Jupiter is almost identical in composition to the Sun. More than 90 percent of it is formed of the two very light gases, hydrogen and helium. Much of the remainder is "icy," being composed of frozen hydrogen compounds of carbon, nitrogen, and oxygen.

In that early period, material was still raining down upon the young Sun, Hills believes, and the Sun shone about thirty times more brightly than now. Furthermore, the infant Sun is thought to have gone through a period in which it shed gas at a tremendous rate. This phenomenon has been observed in other stars. It is called the T Tauri stage after the star of that name in the constellation Taurus, the Bull. The star T Tauri varies radically in brightness (between 9th and 13th magnitude), as do other stars of that type, and is thought to shed great quantities of gas.

Because lightweight or volatile material during this period was largely swept out of the Sun's neighborhood, the inner planets are "Earthy," with abundant heavier elements and very little hydrogen and helium. At this stage, as envisioned by Whipple, Jupiter and Saturn were already formed, and Jupiter generated enough gravity to hold onto all its mate-

rial, including the light gases, as the great wind blew
out from the Sun. Saturn, farther out, with less than
one third the mass of Jupiter, still had enough gravity to retain much of its hydrogen and helium. Beyond that, however, those gases were swept away,
leaving the gases that combine hydrogen with oxygen (water), with nitrogen (ammonia), and with carbon (methane). As a result 85 percent of the outer
planets, Uranus and Neptune, are those gases,
largely in frozen form, 15 percent are the heavier elements with only trace amounts of hydrogen and helium. Whipple proposed that those planets and the
comets are essentially made of the same material.

Comets, it is thought, formed beyond the orbit of
Saturn. Some came together to form "cometesi-
mals"—objects comparable in size to an asteroid—
that, in turn, combined to produce Uranus and
Neptune. Once those planets had taken their final
form, gravitational encounters with the planets scattered the remaining comets hither and yon—some
to die in the Sun, some to fall onto Saturn, some to
vanish into space, and some to populate the Oort
Cloud. Whipple believed, however, that some remained in stable, almost circular orbits not very far
beyond the outermost planets (but much closer than
the Oort Cloud). "But," he said, "they cannot be observed directly as comets, nor by total reflected light
from the Sun, nor by obscuration of stars. So without sending space probes to that region of space, I
think it is hopeless to observe such comets directly,
in case they do exist."

Nevertheless, he proposed that such a comet
cloud could account for peculiarities in the motion
of Neptune that had been attributed to Pluto, the
outermost planet, whose size seemed too small for it
to have played such a role. Another test would be to
see if the path of a comet is affected by a comet
cloud not far beyond the planets. Halley's Comet
seemed the best suited to such a test. S. E. Hamid,

Brian Marsden, and Whipple examined the last two apparitions of that comet and found no evidence for the gravitational effect that such a cloud would have on Halley's path. They concluded that if the cloud exists, its combined mass cannot be greater than that of the Earth.

Another explanation for the special composition of the outer planets, which does not presume such early formation of Jupiter, was proposed by Sir Fred Hoyle in the late 1940s. He suggested that heat as far from the Sun as Uranus and Neptune was still sufficient to "boil off" the lighter gases of the nebula (hydrogen and helium) whereas the gravity of the young Sun at that distance was too weak to keep those gases from flying off into space. Closer in, at the orbital distances of Jupiter and Saturn, solar gravity was still strong enough to retain the lightest gases. Pluto, the outermost planet, does not resemble any of the other outer planets and may be a former moon of Neptune.

Formation of the inner planets began as material within the contracting disk started assembling into ever-larger solid bodies—"planetesimals"—that fought for dominance in their orbital zones, sweeping up rivals until none remained. Only between the orbits of Mars and Jupiter was there insufficient material for one object to dominate and produce a planet. Relics of that unsuccessful effort remain, however, in the form of spherical asteroids and the fragments of their collisions that sometimes fall to Earth as meteorites.

The planets beyond Saturn, in Whipple's view, formed in the same way, but from planetesimals of cometary composition. Jupiter, Saturn, and probably planets that were beyond them then drew on remnants of the nebula to form their own disks— smaller replicas of the disk from which the planets formed—and these condensed into moons or remained as rings, like those of Saturn. Two asteroids became moons of Mars and an object of uncertain origin became a satellite of the Earth. We call it our Moon, but it is relatively large, compared to its parent body, and may have formed elsewhere.

A puzzle of long standing has been why the Sun spins only once a month. This is a small fraction of the speed one would expect if the Sun inherited from the nebula the same rotational energy, or "angular momentum," as the planets. Although the Sun contains most of the mass of the Solar System, its rotation accounts for only 2 percent of the system's angular momentum, the rest being in the planets—chiefly Jupiter. One explanation has been that the rotating Sun, early in its life, exerted a magnetic drag on the planets, transferring its angular momentum to them.

Another proposition is based on the observation that many young stars go through a T Tauri stage in which they shed vast amounts of material. In this way they can also shed much of their rotational energy. Alastair G. W. Cameron, professor of astronomy at Harvard and an authority on the origin of the Solar System, has calculated that a star formed from the collapse of material no more massive than that now within the Sun would not produce enough heat and pressure in the star's core to ignite the nuclear fires. He believes the nuclear reactions did not begin until the Sun had grown to twice its present mass, whereupon it began shedding material at a stupendous rate. The solar wind in that epoch was so fierce that no atmosphere could survive on the inner planets. The atmospheric gases were swept away, as was any remnant of the original nebula. How, then, did Earth's atmosphere get its chance to form? It is now generally accepted that all of the air and water on Earth, including that which now resides in the oceans, came volcanically out of the Earth's interior after the Sun settled down.

In 1984 Thomas Gold of Cornell University, per-

haps the boldest and most provocative of astrophysical theorists, proposed at a Royal Society meeting in
London another explanation for slow rotation of the
Sun. He, too, envisioned a primordial nebula containing far more material than that which now remains in the Solar System. Once part of it became
concentrated enough to have a center of gravity, it
began to contract. A starlike body began forming
within it, but, without nuclear fires in its core fight-
ing against compression, that body was squeezed to
enormous density. It would be like one of the "stellar cinders" left when a star collapses after it has
burned up its fuel, and its gaseous envelope is no
longer held up by outward-flowing heat and radiation. Such a star collapses into a white dwarf, super-
dense neutron star, or—the ultimate contraction—
into a black hole. But in Gold's proposal the central
object, unlike a neutron star, would not be depleted
in nuclear fuel. As material from the nebula continued to fall onto it the central object would rotate at
the speed characteristic of that depth within the
nebula. Finally the pressure and temperature in its
core would be enough to begin fusing hydrogen
atoms and release the energy that makes stars shine.
The star would expand to mature dimensions, and as
it did so, its spin rate would slow, as does that of a
figure skater who "expands" by spreading his arms.
The star's spin rate would then resemble that of the
Sun, whereas motion of the planets would be determined by angular momentum they inherited from
their part of the nebula. The fact that the Sun's spin
axis is tilted more than 7 degrees to the ecliptic,
Gold said, implies that the Sun and planets had separate histories. The comets, he added, were formed so
far out that their motions did not become concentrated in a disk and their orbits are not confined to
the ecliptic.

What makes plausible the entire nebular hypothesis for the origin of the Sun and its planets is the

one-way nature of rotation throughout the system. It is almost universally counterclockwise. That is the direction in which the planets orbit the Sun. The latter spins counterclockwise, as do all the planets except Uranus and Venus; the latter hardly spins at all, being gravitationally locked into a very slow retrograde rotation. All of the true moons, such as the four Galilean moons of Jupiter, also circle their parent planets in the "proper" manner. Jupiter's four inner moons—the largest and brightest ones, discovered by Galileo in 1610—circle that giant planet in the plane of its equator, as would be expected if they were children of a disk that formed from material left over from the planet's own condensation. The outer Jovian moons are in randomly oriented orbits and are thought to be asteroids that came close enough to be captured by Jupiter's gravity.

In 1898, two years after Clarence Day, the author of *Life With Father*, based on his childhood experiences, graduated from Yale, a moon was found to be orbiting Saturn in the "wrong" direction. Christened Phoebe, it was the first moon that seemed to violate the nebular theory, and Day was inspired to compose the following ditty:

> *Phoebe, Phoebe whirling high*
> *In our neatly-plotted sky,*
> *Listen, Phoebe, to my lay:*
> *Won't you whirl the other way?*
>
> *All the other stars are good*
> *And revolve the way they should.*
> *You alone, of that bright throng,*
> *Will persist in going wrong.*
>
> *Never mind what God has said—*
> *We have made a Law instead.*
> *Have you never heard of this*
> *Neb-u-lar Hy-poth-e-sis?*
>
> *It prescribes, in terms exact,*
> *Just how every star should act.*

*Tells each little satellite*
*Where to go and whirl at night.*

*Disobedience incurs*
*Anger of astronomers,*
*Who—you mustn't think it odd—*
*Are more finicky than God.*

*So, my dear, you'd better change*
*Really, we can't rearrange*
*Every chart from Mars to Hebe*
*Just to fit a chit like Phoebe.*

Phoebe, like the outer moons of Jupiter, is probably a captured asteroid. The asteroids, in contrast
with the icy comets, are rocky objects resembling
miniature planets, and most of them circle the Sun
between the orbits of Mars and Jupiter. The comets
also violate the one-way rule and their orbits are
often steeply tilted with reference to those of the
planets. Their orbits might provide clues to the region of their birth, were it not for the likelihood that
the paths they are flying now have no relationship to
their original orbits. If, as is widely believed, a star
now and then plows through the Oort Cloud, scat-
tering comets like a flock of startled birds, the present comet orbits are of little value in that regard.

There remain several possibilities. The most
straightforward explanation would be that the comets originated where they now reside in the Oort
Cloud, flying around the outer limits of the Solar
System, along orbits tilted at all angles to the ecliptic. They would then form a great spherical halo resembling the giant halo of very old stars far outside
the flattened disk of the Milky Way Galaxy. After
those stars formed many billions of years ago from
the spherical cloud that constituted the galaxy at its
earliest stage, the remaining material shrank, its
rotation rate increased, concentrating subsequent
generations of stars, including our Sun, into the

disk-shaped region occupied by the spiral arms. According to Rüdeger Reinhard of the European Space Agency's Giotto mission to Comet Halley, the comets may have had a similar history, they may be a "memory" of the nebula's original spherical shape, as well as unaltered residues of its initial composition. They might even be samples of primordial material that is adrift throughout the vast reaches between stars.

The difficulty with this hypothesis is that astrophysicists like Dr. Hills believe the comets could not have formed as far out from the center of the Solar System as the Oort Cloud. At that distance each particle of the nebula was inches distant from any other particle. The probability that particles would collide and stick together would have been extremely low. Other theorists, however, believe that when newly forming stars, including the Sun, were still close together, the outer part of the solar nebula may have been dense enough for comet formation. Cameron has proposed that comets may have formed in miniature nebulae orbiting the solar nebula and remained there as the Oort Cloud.

One the other hand Fred Whipple, the dean of comet specialists, has argued that the comets could not have formed as close in as the orbits of the outer planets, Uranus and Neptune, for two reasons. The lighter gases known to be abundant in comets would have been swept away by the same process that caused those planets to be depleted in hydrogen and helium. Furthermore the orbital periods of typical comets are too long to be representative of that zone of the Solar System. This has led Hills and others to argue that the comets formed beyond the planets, but well inside the region of the Oort Cloud—specifically between 1,000 and 5,000 astronomical units from the Sun. Pluto is forty such units out, and the Oort Cloud is at about 50,000 units.

What pushed the material together enough to

stick and begin forming tiny "snowflakes" that
evolved into comets, according to Hills, was radiation pressure from the infant Sun pushing outward
and similar inward pressure from the scores of
young stars that were still close at hand. Furthermore, because sunlight was scattered off dust grains
in the cloud, its pressure was likewise exerted from
many directions. The result may have been a cosmic
snowstorm of immense dimensions, contracting at a
rate of perhaps one third of a mile per hour. Hills
believes the cloud from which a typical comet—one
a half mile in diameter—formed was originally 1.8
million miles wide. As external pressure squeezed
it, a snowballing effect ensued until the diameter
shrank to about 17 miles. It was then that the cloud
became dense enough for its own gravity to begin
pulling it together, leading to collapse of the cloud
into the giant "dirty snowball" envisioned by Whipple as the nature of today's comets.

Because a number of comet nuclei have broken
into pieces even while far from their stressful encounters with the Sun, there is a suspicion that they
are formed of smaller accumulations that break
apart more readily than a single icy body.

Many of the comets formed in that intermediate
zone beyond the planets would eventually have been
thrown hither and yon by the gravity of planets or
passing stars. Some would have been thrown out of
the Solar System or toward a fiery death in the Sun.
As many as a million billion, according to some estimates, would have ended up in the Oort Cloud, and
some may still be orbiting the Sun in the region of
their birth, between the Oort Cloud and the planets.

# S I X

An
Anatomy
Lesson

***The Tran-*** What makes comets so spectacular is that they
***quillity—*** know how to dress. Halley's Comet is at its core,
***and the Heat*** according to all the available evidence, a lumpy,
solid mass of no special looks hurtling through the
dark vastness of space. But that core—known as the
nucleus—becomes surrounded by a huge and wonderful glow, the coma, as the comet approaches the
Sun. Then, radiating out from it and often trailing
behind it like the most diaphanous train of the
grandest gown in the universe is Halley's tail.

That brilliant image, seen under good conditions,
is enough to fill the men and women of Earth with
admiration. But there is more to it than that. The
image will change continually, and a grasp of comet
anatomy is of invaluable assistance in the search for
the finer points of cometary drama and beauty.

As Halley's Comet speeds toward Earth, it is also
heading, literally and figuratively, toward its one
moment in the Sun. By far the majority of this and
any comet's life is spent so far from the Sun that it is
not at all luminous. It is generally thought to be a
dull, "dirty snowball" in the words of Harvard's Fred
Whipple, who offered his theory of the nucleus's

115

composition in 1950. The theory says that the comet is composed of dusty ice chiefly made of water but with frozen carbon dioxide, ammonia, and other gases as well. There is some evidence that comets become dimmer after they have made a close passage of the Sun, as though solar heat had melted off much of the surface ice, leaving a predominantly dusty coat.

Before Whipple's explanation came along, many astronomers believed the cores of comets were not a solid, frozen mass, but relatively loose, like a sand pile or gravel bank. In the 1950s, this continued to be the thesis of Britain's Raymond A. Lyttleton, but others argued that the gravity exerted by so small an object as a comet could play no role in holding together such an insubstantial nucleus when it was faced by severe tidal stresses in its first close passage of the Sun. It would be torn apart. (Comets do sometimes break up, but that often occurs long after they have circled the Sun.)

In the dirty snowball model, abundant "dirt" is thought to be embedded within these ices—grains of dust formed from various compounds of carbon, nitrogen, and other elements. No one has ever obtained a good look at such an object because, as the comet enters the inner Solar System, sunlight vaporizes frozen gas on its surface, forming the coma that surrounds and obscures the comet nucleus. That's one more reason why the return of Halley's Comet this time has brought with it such excitement as astronomers hope to determine whether Whipple is correct about the nucleus or, even if he is proved wrong, to learn once and for all the true composition of a comet.

Even the size of the nucleus is not well known now. The nucleus of Halley's Comet is thought to be less than 5 miles in diameter and probably lumpy, since so small an object does not generate enough

**The radio telescope at Arecibo, Puerto Rico, examined Comet Encke in 1980 to estimate its diameter. It was used again as IRAS-Araki-Alcock came by.**

gravity to mold a smooth sphere. On its last apparition, it appeared to be rotating every ten hours.

Radar echoes obtained from the nucleus of Comet Encke in 1980, using the giant dish antenna at Arecibo, Puerto Rico, showed its diameter to lie somewhere between 1,300 and 13,000 feet. In 1983 Comet IRAS-Araki-Alcock passed within 3 million miles of the Earth—our closest encounter with a comet since 1770. Radar probing by the Arecibo antenna showed its shape to be somewhat boxlike and its radius to be only a few miles.

If the spacecraft sent to observe Halley are unable to see the solid nucleus inside its coma, another ap-

proach may shed some light on its size. The Lowell
Observatory in Flagstaff, Arizona, has identified
close to sixty occasions through July 4, 1987, when
the nucleus should pass in front of or close to a
bright star. It is hoped that this will make it possible
to record when the star's light is cut off and when it
reappears, indicating the dimensions of the nucleus.

Although the coma is a profound nuisance to anyone trying to observe the comet's core, it is nevertheless one of Comet Halley's glories. Many comets,
as observed from the Earth, seem to have comas just
barely thick enough to hide the nucleus from view,
but brighter ones, like Halley's, are shrouded in
comas at least a few thousand miles in radius. Some
are huge. This became evident in 1811 when a
comet came into view with a glowing coma 1.25
million miles wide, making it larger than the Sun.

The readily visible coma contains free atoms, a variety of small molecules, and ice-coated grains, the
proportion of dust to gas ranging between 10 and 50
percent. Ultraviolet observations from such satellites as the Orbiting Astronomical Observatory 2
and Orbiting Geophysical Observatory 5, however,
have revealed a tenuous outer coma formed of single
hydrogen atoms that reaches out several million
miles. While the coma, to some extent, resembles a
planetary atmosphere, it is transitory, constantly
blown away by the solar wind and replenished by gas
from the nucleus that blows out at a speed of about
2,000 miles per hour. The gas, in a process called
sublimation, passes directly from the solid to the
gaseous state without going through a liquid stage.

A few comets have been seen so far out that astronomers apparently viewed them before they had
the chance to evolve a coma. These unadorned comets seemed to be shining with sunlight reflected
from their solid surfaces. But little could be learned
about them because they were so distant. Even in
the most powerful telescopes, they appear only as

points of light. If they are "new" comets making their first deep penetration of the Solar System after billions of years in the Oort Cloud, some specialists believe their long exposure to cosmic rays—high-energy radiation raining on them from the cosmos—must have altered their surface material into some form of highly reflective crust. The crust, the thinking goes, is destroyed as the coma forms and the comets near the Sun.

If comets are the most frequently changing components of the Solar System—everything about them subject to change without notice—that is particularly true of their tails. The dramatic variability of the tails was driven home to Earthbound observers as Halley's Comet approached the last time around. As high-quality astronomical photography was developed for the first time soon after the turn of the century, it meant that Halley's tail could be photographed through the most powerful telescopes in unprecedented detail. And, two years before that, in 1908, the tail of Comet Morehouse would also supply exciting evidence of a cometary tail's turbulent life.

Comet tails can be spectacularly dynamic, showing evidence of what may be explosions inside the comet. And the tail does not trail placidly behind a comet like the wake of a ship. Rather it often changes its position, the determining factor being its relationship to the Sun—it is always blown away from the direction of the Sun.

The tails of major comets can assume many forms and sometimes are double, with one tail quite straight and the other curved. The straight tail, reaching in a direction almost directly opposite the Sun, often develops rapidly moving kinks, corkscrews, and lumps that are the delight of observers on Earth. The entire tail may be shed, like a lizard's, whereupon a new one evolves. There are still no generally accepted explanations for these phenom-

In 1908, photos of Comet Morehouse provided dramatic evidence of the turbulence in cometary tails. *(Lick Observatory)*

ena; and, as John C. Brandt of NASA's Goddard Space Flight Center notes, Comet Halley "presents an unparalleled opportunity" for the intensive, coordinated, worldwide observations needed to explain them.

Some tails are amazingly long, given their provenance. After all, they originate in objects usually no more than a few miles wide. A really big comet nucleus might approach 50 miles in diameter. But that is nothing compared to the grandest of tails. One tail, seen in 1843, reached 200 million miles across the Solar System—more than twice the distance of Earth to the Sun. Not all comets, however, produce observable tails. In fact most of those discovered by telescopic searches and reported each year to the international clearinghouse for sightings in Cambridge, Massachusetts, have no tail at all.

Our understanding of comets is severely limited by the fact that we only see a tiny percentage of those thought to exist, and then only during the brief period when they are near enough to the Sun to be illuminated by reflected sunlight and by the action of solar radiation in causing the comet's material to glow, or fluoresce. So an understanding of how tails form and act has been slow in coming. In 1836 Friedrich Wilhelm Bessel proposed that the tail was blown away from a comet by the pressure of sunlight. In the near vacuum of space, such pressure can, for example, alter the path of a hollow, lightweight spacecraft, but this did not seem adequate to explain the enormous comet tails sometimes observed nor the frequent observation of double tails.

The tail known as the plasma tail stretches almost directly away from the Sun, skewed slightly away from that direction by the comet's own motion. Analysis of the light from such tails has shown them to be entirely composed of plasmas—gases (chiefly water vapor and carbon monoxide) stripped of electrons by ultraviolet light from the Sun. The other tail type, known as a dust tail, forms at angles separated from the plasma tail by as much as 60 degrees and can be relatively diffuse.

Both tails are fed by the action of sunlight in causing ices of the nucleus to sublime, releasing gases that fly off in all directions at high velocity. This forms the coma and carries the dust particles that had been embedded within the ice. Then light from the Sun, chiefly at ultraviolet wavelengths, knocks electrons off the gas atoms, making them electrically charged (ionized). Such a gas is susceptible to capture by magnetic fields in gases that blow out from the Sun and past the comet head, dragging the plasma into a tail.

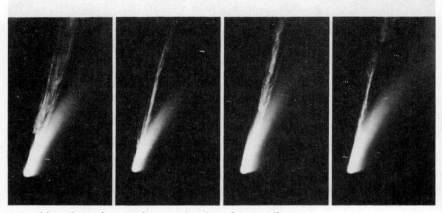

COMET MRKOS

**Double tails are frequently seen. One is a plasma tail, which stretches almost directly away from the sun; the other is a dust tail, formed when the ices in the nucleus are released.**

The dust particles, on the other hand, do not "feel" the magnetism, but respond to two forces: the pressure of sunlight and the Sun's gravity. They therefore remain in orbit around the Sun, but steadily moving away from it, forming the curved dust tail. Infrared emissions from such a tail indicate that most of the particles are tiny—one micron (1 millionth of a meter) in diameter. Although Comet IRAS-Araki-Alcock as seen from Earth in 1983 displayed little or no tail to observers looking at it with the naked eye or conventional equipment, sensors on IRAS—the Infrared Astronomical Satellite, co-discoverer of the comet—charted a dust tail 250,000 miles long. The twelve American, British, and Dutch astronomers responsible for the mission reported that this tail, "which has no counterpart in the visual observations," indicates that the comet head must be giving off dust at a rate of 200 kilograms (400 to 500 pounds) a second—far more than had been suspected and a good deal more, in terms of percentage, than Comet Halley is thought to be losing. The comet, which did not get much closer to the Sun than Earth, is believed to be in a 1,000-year orbit.

Some of the grains ejected by comet heads are apparently so large they remain relatively near the comet, forming an "antitail." The antitail is sometimes seen as a spike resembling the slender tusk of a narwhal that seems to project toward the Sun instead of away from it. It is believed to be composed of grains so heavy they are ejected at low velocity and continue in orbit close to the comet. They form a fan-shaped accumulation in the plane of the comet's own orbit that is so thin that it can only be seen as the Earth crosses that plane. The effect is like that of a disk-shaped halo of dust or smoke that is too thin to be seen except when one's eye is aligned with the disk. Material forming the antitail probably surrounds the comet but can only be seen on the Sun-facing side. It may be large particles such as these that spread along the orbits of some comets and ultimately fall into the Earth's atmosphere as a shower of meteors.

The kinks, waves, knots, and corkscrews in plasma tails can move out along the tail at speeds sometimes exceeding 500,000 miles per hour. It is not certain, however, whether it is actually the cometary material in the tail that is moving so very fast. Rather, in some cases, we may be seeing a wave motion, like the ripples moving along a shaken rope. In any case it was such motions that led the German astronomer Ludwig Biermann in 1951 to propose that the plasma tails are produced by hot gas blowing from the Sun at extremely high velocity. Subsequently the Swedish astrophysicist Hannes Alfvén, who won a Nobel Prize in 1970, suggested that magnetic fields carried in this solar wind picked up the electrified plasma and formed the tail. Evidence for this was found when a magnetic storm on the Sun was followed soon afterward by a disturbance of the Comet Whipple-Fedtke, as though the effect had propagated outward with the hypothetical solar wind.

The plasma tail often splits into rays that may be a half million miles long. Over a period of many hours the rays tend to migrate toward the central axis of the tail and fuse with it. Sometimes the plasma tail breaks loose from the comet and drifts away like the smoke plume from a ship that has stopped its engines. A new tail then begins to form. In a book-length summation of what is known about comets, published by the University of Arizona in 1982, Susan Wyckoff of Arizona State University said seventy-two such "disconnections" had been observed.

John Brandt of NASA pointed out in that volume that an early observation of these phenomena was described in 1908 by W. H. M. Christie, Britain's Astronomer Royal, from observations of Comet Morehouse. Starting from a starlike nucleus and very narrow tail, he wrote, "There is an expansion of the comet which on the side towards the sun forms parabolic envelopes, and these are brought round to the tail, forming a sort of fan-shape; and we note that the angles between the rays of the fan change in the course of a night; then, as time goes on, the fan-shaped streamers coalesce into the tail. We then get a streaming tail which breaks up into flocculent masses and appears to be in a state of great disturbance, and this goes off apparently into space and the comet starts fresh again."

The journal *Observatory*, reporting on the same apparition, said: "The formation of the tail seems to be intermittent rather than continuous. There seem to be at intervals convulsions or explosions in the nucleus, producing big bunches or lumps of tail which travel away and leave the comet with a small tail for a time." During the last apparition of Halley's Comet a similar "detachment event" was photographed in its tail on May 13, 1910.

In 1957 Alfvén proposed an explanation for some of these phenomena that has been reinforced by observations from space probes and elaborated by Brandt. It has long been known that clouds of gas embedded in vast, looping magnetic fields are thrown out by the Sun. Such phenomena have been recorded on film as high-arching "prominences" of fiery-red gas that soar from the edge of the Sun. Most such prominences then fall back, but some, as recorded in Skylab observations from space, fly off into space. Once the concept of a solar wind blowing out past the planets became established, it was assumed that such looping magnetic fields ride with the wind. As the Sun rotated, it appeared to be ejecting successive magnetic loops, like jets from a rotating lawn sprinkler, that periodically sweep past the comet head. Beginning in the 1960s this was repeatedly confirmed by magnetic recordings on deep space probes. Each time they crossed a boundary between such loops the recorded magnetic field reversed direction, or "polarity."

As described by Brandt, when the solar wind and the magnetic field lines embedded within it encounter the thin atmosphere around the comet head, a shock front is formed like the one ahead of a supersonic aircraft. The wind and its magnetic field lines wrap themselves around the comet head, sweeping away some of its atmosphere to form a wake. This wake, like other plasmas, is electrically charged, its visible constituents consisting chiefly of carbon monoxide. When the solar wind throws a new magnetic domain against the comet's bow shock front, the magnetic polarity is reversed; new magnetic loops begin to form, the tail is detached, and a tail based on the new polarity is formed.

A magnetic tail also forms as the solar wind

sweeps past Earth (or more precisely past the domain under control of Earth's magnetism in nearby
space). Swept out on the downwind side of Earth, it
may reach past the orbit of the Moon. The magnetism, however, does not derive from the wind; it is
an elongation of Earth's own magnetic field. Comet
heads, unlike Earth, are not believed to carry any intrinsic magnetism, apart from that induced in them
by the solar wind.

A major uncertainty will be the location of the
bow shock in front of Halley's Comet. As pointed
out by Rüdeger Reinhard of the European Space
Agency, whose spacecraft, Giotto, is designed to
penetrate the shock front and pass 300 miles upwind
of the comet head, "We don't even know if a bow
shock exists. We could be inside or outside of it. We
have to be prepared for big surprises." The best guess
is that the shock front will be encountered about
60,000 miles out, and particles of the coma will begin bombarding the spacecraft at a distance of some
400 miles (one hour before closest approach). Reinhard has told a press conference that Giotto's plasma
detection experiment would probably be turned on
several hours in advance to be sure it did not miss
the crossing of the shock front.

The "explosions" observed in comet heads and
other events that send sharp bends, twists, and
knots racing down the tail may all be induced by
sudden magnetic changes. One of the surprises from
observations close to Venus has been that after the
solar wind hits its atmosphere, long "ropes" of
twisted magnetism form behind the resulting shock
front—an effect that could be related to the corkscrews sometimes seen in comet tails. In 1976 a
kink was photographed moving along the tail of
Comet West at more than 200,000 miles per hour,
but there is still no agreement on whether this was
motion of the plasma or a wave phenomenon. Furthermore there is no accepted theory to explain why

some comets have both dust tail and plasma tail, some have only a prominent plasma tail, and others are largely limited to a dust tail. At its last apparition Halley's had both kinds of tail and probably will do so again.

Noting how far astronomers are from understanding such phenomena, Brandt quotes the American astronomer, Edward Emerson Barnard, author of some 900 papers and an avid comet hunter during the late nineteenth and early twentieth centuries: "The changes from day to day in the comet are so very great that it is usually not possible to connect certainly any phenomenon of one night with that of the night before, as no part of the tail would be likely to live over the interval." The rapid changes characteristic of comets, yet rarely recorded because of limited observing times, were illustrated when Comet Bradfield was photographed on February 6, 1980, by the Joint Observatory for Cometary Research, South Baldy, New Mexico. Its tail was found to have noticeably changed direction in less than a half hour, presumably in response to a shift in the solar wind.

The prospect of many closely spaced observations is yet another reason that astronomers have such great expectations for the Halley return.

*Self-Propelled and Self-Destructive Comets* Although, broadly speaking, comets appear to be in free flight along paths controlled entirely by the gravity of the Sun and planets, when they are closely observed, it becomes evident that other forces are at work and sometimes they even seem to "explode" into fragments. These other forces appear to be the same explosions thought by some to play havoc with the cometary tail. As Zdenek Sekanina, a leading specialist on such behavior, has put it: "Comets are prone to self-destruction."

He points out that early in the nineteenth century

the German astronomer T. F. Encke noticed "something fishy" about the orbit of what is now called Comet Encke. When he examined old records of comet sightings, he concluded that those observed in 1786, 1795, and 1805 were all the same object, orbiting the Sun in the shortest time of any comet known then or now, namely every 3.3 years. It would, he said, return in 1822, and it did so. But according to Encke's very careful calculations, it was two hours ahead of schedule. He concluded that something was robbing it of orbital energy, making its orbit smaller.

The same effect is seen on Earth satellites as they dip into the atmosphere. They begin to drop lower; their orbital velocity increases, but their orbits shrink as a prelude to their final plunge. Encke lived in an era when astronomers believed space to be filled with an invisible "ether" through which light waves propagate like sound waves through the air or other material. It was drag exerted by this ether, he thought, that was shortening the orbit of his comet. He introduced an arbitrary correction into calculations of Comet Encke's periodic apparitions, but when, late in the century, his corrections became inadequate and the ether was shown to be nonexistent, some other explanation had to be found. Not only was the orbit of Encke changing, but so were those of other short-period comets. Some, like that of Encke, were contracting, but others were getting larger.

The influence of some force other than gravity on the orbits of more than three dozen comets has now been demonstrated, thanks largely to the detailed calculations of Brian Marsden at the Smithsonian Astrophysical Observatory in Cambridge, Massachusetts, as well as by Donald K. Yeomans and Sekanina at the California Institute of Technology's Jet Propulsion Laboratory in Pasadena. Yeomans and Tao Kiang of Dunsink Observatory in Ireland have analyzed European and Chinese records of Halley's returns from 1404 B.C. until the present. They found a consistent effect of nongravitational forces on its orbit at least as far back as A.D. 837, when the comet was very close to the Earth—within 4 million miles —providing Yeomans and Kiang with a highly precise starting point from which to retrace its orbital history.

The explanation for the mysterious force at work on such comets came in 1950 with Fred Whipple's proposition that comets are "dirty snowballs." When such an object is near enough to the Sun for sunlight to sublime frozen gases on its surface, those gases fly off with enough energy to affect the comet's flight path, assuming the ejection is not uniform in all directions. The sublimation would occur on the Sun-facing side of the comet, but if that side then rotated away from the Sun's direction before the resulting jet of expelled gas could gain momentum, the resulting direction of thrust would depend on the axis of rotation. It would also be affected by where on the surface of the comet's nucleus the jet originated. It appears that parts of the surface are more volatile than others, so that the jets originate in specific areas, like the thrusters and rocket nozzles on a spacecraft that point in many directions so its orientation and its motion through space can be controlled. Each comet probably has its own pattern of orbital changes due to such gas jets. In some cases, particularly with such short-period comets as Brorsen, Comas Sola, Finlay, and Kopff, the behavior seems extremely variable. Whipple has attributed this in part to toppling of the spin axes caused by changes in the shape of the nucleus as material is lost from specific parts of it. When the spin tumbles or wobbles, like a dying top, the jets keep changing their aim.

He and Sekanina have done an intensive study of the seemingly erratic changes in Comet Encke during its fifty-nine apparitions between 1786 and 1977. During that time the spin axis of the comet seems to have flipped almost completely over. The two astronomers have confirmed that behavior of its jets is highly sensitive to even slight changes in orientation of the comet's spin axis relative to the plane of its orbit. The spin axis of Encke is currently such that, when the comet approaches the Sun, its axis lies parallel to its orbital plane, and one pole is aimed at the Sun. One hemisphere is therefore continuously exposed to sunlight and the other is continuously in darkness. Dust and larger fragments boil (are sublimed) off the Sun-facing side and accumulate on the opposite hemisphere, building up a mantle that protects the ice beneath it when next exposed to sunlight.

Thus only certain parts of the surface produce jets. "Peculiar" variations observed in the brightness of Encke occur, Sekanina and Whipple said, because the sublimation rate is "highly dependent" on which area of the comet is facing the Sun. Such sensitivity to even slight changes in the relationship between spin axis and orbital plane explains why comets behave in such strange ways as they come close enough to Jupiter for the planet's gravity to alter that relationship. They estimated the mass of Encke to be about 10 billion tons and that 0.09 percent of it is shed on each passage around the Sun.

The splitting of comets into as many as five fragments is less easy to explain, although the same kind of jets may be involved. So far, twenty-two splitters have been identified, although in no case was the moment of splitting observed, and that may never become possible unless a spacecraft is nearby at the critical moment. The most recent discovery of a splitter was that of Comet Du Toit–Hartley, first sighted in 1945 and rediscovered in 1982 by Malcolm Hartley at the United Kingdom's Schmidt Telescope in Siding Spring, Australia. It turned out that two fragments, although many hours apart, were flying essentially the same orbit.

Sekanina has sought to deduce what causes such comets to break up. The obvious explanation would be tidal or thermal stresses as they whip around the Sun, but this does not fit most of the observations. The splits seem to occur at random points in their orbits. In about half the cases, it happens before they come near the Sun, rather than afterward. In one such case, the approaching comet was almost as far out as Saturn. Only five of thirty-two fragments studied by Sekanina separated from their parent bodies while under tidal stress because they were close to the Sun or Jupiter. Two of the fragmenting comets were "Sun-grazers": the Great September Comet of 1882 and Comet Ikeya-Seki of 1965.

When a comet splits, both the resulting fragments may develop tails and in all respects resemble the original comet, although smaller. This is regarded by some as evidence that the internal structure of comets is fairly uniform. In other cases a "parent" sheds smaller fragments that tend to move along the tail and disintegrate.

By plotting the rate at which the fragments are separating from one another or their assumed "parent," the time of rupture has been estimated, and in some cases records show that the comet flared up at that moment, either in brightness or in a cloud of dust that then moves along the tail. This led to the hypothesis that the comet was blown apart by some sort of explosion, but according to Sekanina the rates of separation are less than one mile per hour—hardly consistent with a violent rupture—and the trajectories of the fragments indicate that they are to some extent self-propelled. When the motions of several fragments are run backward, like reversing a moving picture, they do not converge on the parent body in the way expected if they were merely thrown out by an explosion. That the fragments are

The same explosions thought to be responsible for turbulence in a comet's tail are believed to cause some comets to burst apart. A series of photos shows the fragmenting of Comet West. *(New Mexico State University Observatory)*

propelled by jets of gas sublimed from their surfaces is also suggested by the manner in which such propulsion weakens at greater distances from the Sun. It does so roughly in step with the weakening of sunlight at such increasing distances, implying dependence of the jets on solar heating.

Nor is an event of great violence probably necessary to cause a split. The mass of a comet is so small that it does not produce enough gravity to bind the nucleus strongly together. Ernst Öpik, an Estonian-born astronomer at Armagh Observatory in Ireland, has calculated that two disintegrating Sun grazers were made of material no stronger than meteoritic dust balls.

Another hypothesis is that comets fly apart because of fast rotation. Whipple has done the definitive analysis of comet rotations, whose rates can be estimated by observing jets radiating from their nuclei, by recording alteration of their light wavelengths by their rotary motion—the so-called Doppler effect—or by observation of halos periodically ejected from the nucleus. The average spin rate for forty-seven comets proved to be fifteen hours, whereas that for forty-one small asteroids was 6.8 hours. From the relatively slow rate of comet spins, Whipple concluded that the comets were formed by very gradual accumulation whereas the asteroids, probably being fragments of larger bodies, inherited their spin from the collisions that knocked them loose. "It appears that the comets aggregated in a more quiescent region of space than the asteroids, or at least were less disturbed by collisional effects," Whipple wrote in 1982.

He proposed that only one split comet, Honda 1955 V, seems to have been spinning fast enough to be torn apart by centrifugal force. He pointed out, however, that its rotation rate of 4.14 hours was not well established. He also found little support for another possibility, namely that heat generated by radioactive material within the comet was enough to melt part of its "snow," causing the comet to shrink and therefore increase its spin rate until it broke apart. Whipple, however, has discussed the possibility that, during prolonged residence in outer space, volatile material driven out from the comet's interior by radioactive heating solidified there into a rigid crust, which held the comet together until sunlight destroyed the crust and allowed the comet to split.

An explanation for splitting favored by Sekanina is based on the observation that the spin axes of a surprising number of short-period comets are so oriented that, as is currently the case with Encke, they keep one polar region pointed toward the Sun. Material boiled off that hemisphere builds up a thick mantle on the opposite side until the comet becomes so lopsided it breaks apart.

It is conceivable that Halley's Comet will shed an offspring during its current apparition and that the intense observations being conducted from the Earth and from space will help resolve the frustrating problem of what makes at least some comets "self-destructive."

When Halley's comes by this time it will, heaven *The Seeds of* knows, be carrying enough human freight in the *Life* form of mysteries, myths, and portents. Add to all of that the idea that it is a representative of the heavenly bodies that may be responsible for life on Earth. That, at least, is the brunt of one proposal that has spurred considerable thought in recent years.

Between the early 1960s and into the 1980s, Sir Fred Hoyle and his colleague N. C. Wickramasinghe, an authority on interstellar dust, developed the hypothesis that comets carry the seeds of life, ready to evolve whenever cometary material falls into a fertile environment. They argued, in effect, that our most distant ancestors arrived inside one or more comets and that virus particles in meteors—cometary debris falling into the atmosphere—could be responsible for outbreaks of disease against which we have no resistance, such as the global epidemic, or pandemic, of influenza that cost millions of lives in 1918. The wavelengths of infrared heat radiation from interstellar dust, they said, appear "uncannily similar" to those from the cellulose in bacterial cell walls, plant stems, and tree trunks. Comets sweep up such dust grains and, they believe, sometimes deliver them to Earth.

The idea that bacterial spores or viruses might be adrift throughout the galaxy would have been dismissed out of hand were Hoyle not a distinguished scientist who had helped explain how the elements of which the universe—and ourselves—are formed came into being. Hoyle and Wickramasinghe argued that the age of the Earth was not great enough to allow for all the low-probability events needed to evolve the complex processes of life.

It was not the first proposition that life came from elsewhere. Early in this century Svante August Arrhenius in Sweden, winner of the 1903 Nobel Prize in chemistry, argued that spores of life are adrift throughout the universe. Doubts were expressed regarding this so-called panspermia hypothesis because of the severe radiation to which such spores would be exposed in space. Nevertheless it was revived in recent years by two scientists at the Salk Institute in La Jolla, California: Leslie E. Orgel and Francis H. C. Crick of Britain. Crick, a Nobel laureate (physiology, 1962), helped decipher the twisted structure of DNA, the substance responsible for heredity and the continuity of life.

A less radical role for comets than that of Hoyle and Wickramasinghe was proposed in 1961 by Joan Oro, a Spanish-born biologist at the University of Houston in Texas. Comets, he said, provided the Earth with much of the material that made it possible for life to originate on this planet. He calculated that, during the first 2 billion years of the Earth's history, from 200 million to 1,000 billion tons of cometary material enriched the Earth's surface with organic molecules that then became organized into living organisms. Originally the Earth is thought to have been devoid of any atmosphere or surface water. The prevalent view is that, over billions of years, all its air and water were volcanically erupted from within the planet. Some scientists, however, believe falling comets may also have been a major source.

We have no direct knowledge of the chemical composition and size of dust grains (or rocks) inside comet nuclei. By the time such material can be observed from Earth it has been carried out into the coma by gases driven off the comet's surface by solar heat. The material is immediately broken up into atoms or simple compounds by solar radiation (chiefly ultraviolet light). The detected elements, however, are those most abundant throughout the universe (and in living tissue): hydrogen, carbon, nitrogen, and oxygen. Present in lesser quantities are the more common metals. The tally resembles the catalog of substances from which the Solar System is thought to have been formed before the elements were sorted out by the processes that produced the Sun and planets.

The larger asteroids, for example, seem to have evolved in somewhat the same manner as the Earth, becoming sufficiently molten for their heavier components to sink and form an iron core. Stony and iron meteorites are presumably fragments of one or more such bodies. Comets were presumably never large enough for any sorting-out process to occur. As pointed out by Susan Wyckoff of Arizona State University, those arriving freshly from the Oort Cloud do not seem to have been altered by either external or internal activity. They represent, she believes, "the purest samples" remaining from the primordial nebula.

What we know about cometary composition has largely been determined by analysis of light from the comet's fuzzy coma and tail. One of the wonders of astronomy is how much can be learned about a celestial object by analyzing its light. Because atoms and molecules give off or absorb characteristic wavelengths as they receive or shed energy, it is possible, for example, to determine the surface composition of a star billions of miles away. Likewise the temperature, motion, and magnetism of the light source can be learned.

In a sense such analysis—spectroscopy—was born in 1666 when Sir Isaac Newton allowed a beam of sunlight from a hole in a window shade to shine into a glass prism, breaking it up into its rainbow colors. The significance of those colors was not realized, however, until the nineteenth century. Between 1800 and 1802 it was found that when sunlight was thus divided, a thermometer was heated when placed beyond the red end of the artificial rainbow, demonstrating the existence of invisible light in the form of infrared rays or heat radiation. Beyond the opposite end of the visible spectrum, it was found that unseen rays darkened silver chloride, indicating the presence of ultraviolet light. The critical step, however, was taken in midcentury when Gustav Robert Kirchhoff of Germany, working with Robert Bunsen, showed that the chemical composition of a light source can be determined from the multiple lines of its spectrum, since those lines represent wavelengths of absorption or emissions characteristic of each constituent. Kirchhoff applied this method to the Sun, and in 1864, the Italian astronomer Giovanni Battista Donati was the first to aim a spectroscope at a comet.

Since comets only become visible as they near the Sun, he assumed all of their luminosity would come from reflected sunlight and that he would therefore record only the solar spectrum. Instead it was evident that substances in the comet were fluorescing—reradiating solar energy at wavelengths indicative of their own composition. Through such spectroscopic techniques, a great deal has been learned about the makeup of at least those parts of the comet that can be viewed directly—the coma and tail. As noted earlier, the composition of the unseen nucleus has been deduced from that of the material boiled off it.

While comets differ widely in appearance, their elemental composition is remarkably homogeneous. Infrared light, chiefly at a wavelength of 10 microns (10 millionths of a meter), is scattered off dust tails with high efficiency, indicating that most of the dust grains are very small—about one micron in diameter. Some, however, appear larger than 30 microns and are thought to be silicate grains. Silicates are compounds containing silicon and oxygen, as in quartz, and may also include a variety of other elements. The crust of the Earth is largely formed of silicate rocks. Some microwave emissions from comets have also been attributed to icy grains almost a half inch wide. As noted earlier, it is the larger grains that are thought responsible for anti-tails.

A recent list of constituents observed in cometary comas included carbon, cyanogen, carbon dioxide, carbon monoxide, water, hydroxyl, hydrogen cyanide, gaseous nitrogen, atomic hydrogen, sulfur, sodium, potassium, calcium, vanadium, manganese, iron, cobalt, nickel, and copper. This tally, as noted by Hoyle and Wickramasinghe, includes many of the substances detected, from their telltale radio emissions, in the dust clouds of distant nebulae. But since they are more remote from sources of damaging radiation than a cometary coma newly exposed to sunlight, those distant clouds also contain dozens of more complex molecules, raising the possibility that they also inhabit the protected interior of comets. They include such familiar organic compounds as formaldehyde, formic acid (found in bee stings and red ants), methyl alcohol (poisonous), and ethyl alcohol (the kind in cocktails). At least one eleven-atom molecule has been detected, and several with nine atoms, including dimethyl ether, cyanotriacetylene, and ethyl cyanide.

These compounds, built on skeletons of carbon atoms, are called organic, because it was originally thought they could only be produced by life processes. Virtually all scientific theories on the origin of life see them as the starting material for some form of chemical evolution.

According to the Hoyle-Wickramasinghe hypothesis, comets have icy cores of simple substances, such as water, methane, hydrogen cyanide, and hydrogen sulfide, but have scooped up great quantities of more complex compounds including those detected by radio astronomers in distant dust clouds. The icy core is therefore enveloped in a thick, icy mantle rich in organic substances. At depths exceeding 1,000 feet within this mantle chemical reactions among these compounds heat and melt the frozen gases (chiefly water), forming a small internal "sea" within which, during the millions of years in which a comet wanders through distant space or inhabits the Oort Cloud, chemical evolution can lead to the emergence of bacteria or viruses.

The most widely cited environment for evolution of the first living cell, championed originally by Charles Darwin, is a warm pond filled with a "primordial soup" rich in organic compounds. Hoyle and Wickramasinghe see such a soup forming a "laboratory" inside a comet, shielded from radiation and kept at a stable temperature for millions of years. "It was in such laboratories, a thousand million or more of them, that we shall suppose life in the solar system to have begun," they wrote in 1981.

When a comet is thrown into the inner Solar System and begins a series of close encounters with the Sun, layer upon layer of its surface is melted away. Its inner sea cools as the comet leaves the Sun's vicinity, and the life spores within it go into a "deep freeze" until the comet begins to break up. Some frozen fragments then plunge to Earth as meteors. If they are large enough to protect the bacterial spores or viruses within them from radiation in space and from the heat of passage through the atmosphere, the immigrants could survive.

The survival rate could be extremely small. "The safe arrival of even a few living cells," they wrote, "would have carried the Earth across a huge chasm of biochemical evolution, a chasm which would otherwise be well-nigh impossible to bridge." Subsequent arrivals, they believe, have caused epidemics and are bound to do so again. They even predict reinfection of the world by smallpox bacteria, despite the success of the World Health Organization's smallpox eradication program. Furthermore, genetic material brought to Earth in this manner could promote the sudden evolutionary changes that seem to have occurred.

While such arguments of Hoyle and Wickrama-singhe have won over few of their scientific colleagues, there is evidence that early stages of the chemical evolution which they postulate for cometary interiors have, in fact, occurred beyond the Earth. This has become evident from examination of the earthy, sometimes oily material found in a class of meteorites known as carbonaceous chondrites. Because such meteorites are quickly dissolved by rain, apart from some recent finds in Antarctica, samples have been limited to those picked up immediately after falling to Earth.

Early in the nineteenth century the great Swedish chemist J. Jakob Berzelius examined the first known sample of a carbonaceous chondrite and found its composition so similar to humus that he wondered whether or not it indicated "the presence of organisms on extraterrestrial bodies." As additional specimens fell to Earth and were collected, other chemists had similar thoughts. In 1960 Melvin Calvin of the University of California at Berkeley, a 1961 Nobel laureate, presented to the First International Space Science Symposium, held in Nice, France, a paper coauthored by himself and Susan K. Vaughn entitled, "Extraterrestrial life: some organic constituents of meteorites and their possible significance for extraterrestrial biological evolution." It described some of their analytical results, using high-precision mass spectrometry. The following year Bartholomew Nagy and Douglas J. Hennessy of Fordham University and Warren G. Meinschein of the Esso Research and Engineering Company described their analysis of material from the Orgueil meteorite, a carbonaceous chondrite that fell on France in the previous century. One of them told a reporter: "We believe that wherever this meteorite originated something lived." It was then reported that Frederick D. Sisler of the United States Geological Survey was cultivating living bacteria extracted from a meteorite. He warned, however, that the bacteria could have penetrated the porous specimen after it arrived.

The climax came in November 1961, when Nagy and George Claus of New York University reported finding what appeared to be fossil algae in four separate meteorites. The most strikingly lifelike was a six-sided specimen with tubular protrusions from three sides. Scientists throughout the world rushed to their microscopes. Researchers in Britain, Canada, Hungary, and the Soviet Union all reported similar finds. Then the swelling balloon of excitement burst. It was shown that the six-sided "fossil" was suspiciously like a ragweed pollen grain and it became generally accepted that all the finds were either nonbiological or contaminants. When a meteorite enters the atmosphere after long residence in the near vacuum of space, it powerfully sucks air into its innermost pores, as well as any airborne pollen grains.

Thus the tantalizing prospect that meteorites are fragments of a planet where life once existed fell apart, but analysis of the carbonaceous chondrites has shown that they contain a wide variety of hydrocarbons formed in space by, it is thought, the same process used to synthesize gasoline. They hold, as well, some of the most critical building blocks of life. These include amino acids such as those from which all proteins are assembled. More than fifteen of them have been detected in carbonaceous chondrites that fell on North America, Australia, Asia, and Antarctica. Included are a number found in proteins, although the most abundant meteorite forms are not typical of plant and animal tissues. The Orgueil meteorite has also yielded substances, such as adenine and guanine, that encode the genetic messages in DNA, making possible the continuity of life. Chinese scientists have detected porphyrins in a meteorite that fell in Jilin (Kirin) Province in

1976. Porphyrins are the parent compounds for such
essential biological substances as the hemoglobin
that transports oxygen in the blood and the green
chlorophyll that enables plants to use solar energy
and grow.

Some of these substances may have formed within
the relatively warm environment of the evolving
solar nebula, but others could be relics of more
primitive material of which the comets are also
composed. Such a link between comets and carbonaceous chondrites has been suggested by analysis of particles, including some thought to have
come from comets, collected by high-flying aircraft.
It has long been known that a steady rain of particles
from space falls to the Earth, accumulating, for example, in sea-floor sediments. It is estimated that
10,000 tons of it are swept up each year as the Earth
circles the Sun. Some presumably comes from the
thin, lens-shaped cloud of particles spread uniformly
through the ecliptic—the flattened region within
which the planets and asteroids circle the Sun.

Under ideal seeing conditions at low latitudes,
this dust can be seen with the naked eye forming a
faintly glowing pyramid on the western horizon just
after sunset in spring or in the east just before an
autumn sunrise—times when the path of the ecliptic, marked by the signs of the zodiac, stands per-
pendicular to the horizon. The ancient Egyptians
viewed this phenomenon, known as the zodiacal
light, as some form of divine manifestation, but because it can normally be seen only from locations
between the Tropics of Cancer and Capricorn, it was
unknown to European scientists until the seventeenth century. In 1974 physicists from the Air
Force Geophysics Laboratory in Massachusetts flew
a rocket from the Woomera Test Range in Australia
as part of an Air Force project to catalog infrared
sources throughout the sky. The project's purpose
was probably to avoid mistaking natural sources of

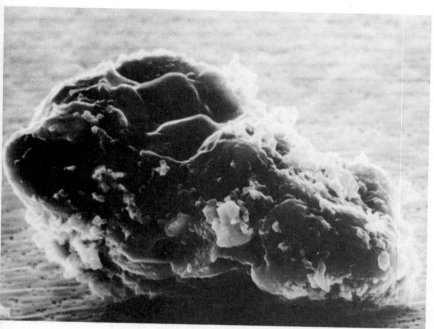

A tiny particle of dust, magnified 15,000 times, believed to have descended from a passing comet. *(NASA)*

infrared radiation for those of military interest, such as rocket engines. Hence a good deal of what was learned during the 1983 mission of IRAS, the international Infrared Astronomical Satellite, was already in the secret archives of the Air Force. However, three participants in the Air Force project, S. D. Price, T. L. Murdock, and L. P. Marcotte, reported in 1980 on the rocket's observation of infrared emissions from the zodiacal light. The results, according to Edward P. Ney of the University of Minnesota, showed that the combined infrared and visible components of light reflected from the dust were much like light reflected from comet grains. This, however, did not prove that all dust in the zodiacal cloud comes from comets. Instead, it could be that the dust in comets and in the zodiacal cloud has a common origin, perhaps in interstellar space.

The collection of dust falling into the Earth's atmosphere became possible thanks to military efforts to collect atomic bomb debris and perform high-altitude reconnaissance. This led to development of U-2 aircraft that could fly above all forms of interception at that time and could collect radioactive particles produced by bomb tests in the atmosphere. Analysis of such particles told much about what nuclear weapons developers in other countries were up to.

The man chiefly responsible for capturing particles falling from space has been Donald E. Brownlee, professor of astronomy at the University of Washington, and they are now widely known as Brownlee particles. They can be collected relatively intact, without having been altered by high temperature, because of their small size. Those less than 0.1 millimeter in diameter, although they enter the highest, thinnest part of the atmosphere at velocities as high as 70,000 miles per hour, are heated slowly because of their very small mass and radiate the heat away before melting. Beginning in 1974 the NASA Ames Research Center in Mountain View, California, began a series of high-flying missions with a U-2 aircraft carrying sticky plastic plates that were not exposed to the air until the plane was more than twelve miles above the Earth.

In 1984 more than 500 particles believed to be of extraterrestrial origin had been collected, and a special laboratory had been created as part of the facility at the Johnson Space Center near Houston built to harbor specimens brought back from the Moon. Each particle is photographed and described in a catalog available to researchers throughout the world.

At least 80 percent of them, according to Dr. Brownlee, are chemically similar to carbonaceous chondrites. Many appear as black, porous clumps of very tiny crystals whose chemistry "closely resembles that of the primitive carbonaceous chondrite meteorites," he reported, "but their structure and mineral composition are different from all other known extraterrestrial materials." Many are so porous and fragile that they could not possibly survive a plunge through the denser atmosphere. The amount of helium they have absorbed from the solar wind and their population of atoms made radioactive by exposure to radiation in space (cosmic rays) show that some have spent at least a million years adrift in space as tiny particles before falling into the atmosphere. They clearly did not come from recent disintegration of such large bodies as comets or meteorites.

The rate at which Earth is sweeping up Brownlee particles is about what one would expect if their origin was the zodiacal cloud. Ney has calculated that Comet Kohoutek shed 20 million tons of dust on its visit to the inner Solar System in 1973–74 and that 5,000 such visits would be enough to replenish the zodiacal cloud. Considering the rate at which the dust is thought to be spiraling in toward the Sun, Dr. Ney calculated that one such comet apparition per year should be enough to replace the losses. The dust falls into the Sun because of a subtle process known as the Poynting-Robertson effect. Any tiny particle in orbit around the Sun absorbs solar energy from a single direction—that of the Sun—but reradiates it in all directions, robbing the particle of orbital momentum. While the pressure of sunlight pushes the particle outward from the Sun, this is not enough to overcome its loss of momentum, and it slowly spirals in toward the Sun. Those now orbiting at the distance from the Sun of the Earth's orbit will take about 7,000 years to spiral inward.

Particles from the zodiacal cloud may contain organic material like that which, some believe, enriched the young Earth and made possible the origin of life. However, they have been too long exposed to space radiation for survival of any germs. Fresher cometary debris drops into the atmosphere at specific times of the year as the Earth, in its orbital flight, passes through trains of debris left by a comet along its own orbit. Such passages produce the meteor showers that sometimes provide dramatic displays of "shooting stars." Since the meteors in each shower are in similar orbits, all those in that shower appear to radiate from the same constellation, and most of the showers are named for that constellation. The Andromedids, for example, appear to come from the constellation Andromeda.

The most prominent meteor showers, their associated comets, and occurrence dates are

April 21: Lyrids (Comet 1861 I)

May 4–6: Eta Aquarids (Comet Halley?)

June 29: Beta Taurids (Comet Encke)

August 12: Perseids [Comet 1862 III]

October 10: Draconids or Giacobinids [Comet Giacobini-Zinner]

October 17–24: Orionids [Comet Halley?]

November 3–10: Taurids [Comet Encke]

November 16: Leonids [Comet Tempel-Tuttle]

November 27: Andromedids [Comet Biela]

December 13: Geminids ["Asteroid" 1983 TB]

# SEVEN

# Race
# for the
# Comet

**Will the
Mysteries Be
Solved?** Some photons traversing more than 1 billion miles of space arrived at Earth October 16, 1982, and registered a faint impression on a silicon-chip sensor near the base of the great 200-inch telescope on Mount Palomar. These particles of radiant energy, from sunlight reflected off a vagabond chunk of dirty ice, carried a message for the astronomers who took notice. The most celebrated comet of all, Halley's Comet, was now back in view.

Since 1977, most large telescopes in the world had been aimed from time to time at the region of the sky just north of the star Procyon, seeking the first sighting of the comet. It was last seen in May of 1911 as it traveled back to the fringes of solar space. Out there in 1948, in the emptiness 3.2 billion miles away, the comet had reached the outer limit of its elongated, cigar-shaped orbit and, responding to the leash of solar gravity, had swung about and begun its return trip. The comet was coming back, everyone felt sure. Its predictability is Halley's most notable attribute. But some comets are thrown off course and become "lost," because of orbital perturbations induced by the larger planets. Astronomers wanted

(Above) The mirror of the Palomar telescope.
(Opposite) The first data on Comet Halley as it returned
was obtained by the 200-inch reflector telescope on Palomar
Mountain on October 16, 1982. *(Union Pacific Railroad)*

to begin tracking Halley's as soon as possible to con-
firm or correct their calculations of its Sunward
course. They were also, not least of all, reacting to
Halley's incomparable tugging on human emotions.
Each astronomer wanted to be first to see the comet.
"It's important to confirm the orbit," said Edwin
Barker, a University of Texas astronomer who had
been straining to see Halley's for several years. "But

there's also a lot of pride involved in being the first
observatory to spot it."

Palomar, long the most powerful optical telescope
in the world, won this minor but spirited race. Two
observers from the California Institute of Technology, G. Edward Danielson and David C. Jewitt,
detected the point of magnified light in the photographs taken through the telescope. The wonder is
that it could be seen at all. The comet, still beyond
the orbit of Saturn then and traveling 23,600 miles
an hour, was as faint as the light from a single candle
seen 27,000 miles away. There was nothing to the
comet but its unprepossessing nucleus; no glowing
coma yet, no double tail of gases and dust, nothing
to hint of the spectacle the comet would become as
it drew closer to the Sun's warming rays. Within two
months, Halley's Comet was picked up at Arizona's
Kitt Peak National Observatory, at the Canada-
France-Hawaii telescope in Hawaii, and at the European Southern Observatory in La Silla, Chile.
Halley's Comet had, as astronomers say, been recovered.

The sightings set in motion long-laid plans for one
of the most intensive investigations of a heavenly
object in the history of astronomy. All the major
telescopes, and the lesser ones, too, would be watching Halley's Comet through every step in its course.
Amateur astronomers by the thousands were being
mobilized round the world. Sounding rockets, high-
altitude aircraft, and balloons were readied for de-
ployment when the comet made its closest approach
to the Earth and the Sun. And for the first time,
there would be an effort to meet the comet halfway,
as it were. A greeting party of four spacecraft was to
be sent forth to rendezvous with it.

Scientists have every reason to believe that the
view they get, through telescopes and spacecraft,
will be the best they have ever had of a comet. In
1910, the world's largest telescope, at Mount Wilson

near Los Angeles, had a 60-inch mirror. Now there are sixteen optical telescopes 96 inches or larger, not to mention the many new telescopes for observations in the wavelengths from radio through the infrared to the ultraviolet, wavelengths that were "invisible" at the time Halley's last appeared. As Ray L. Newburn, Jr., an astronomer at the Jet Propulsion Laboratory, remarked, "In 1910, we were limited to the eyeball and the photographic plate."

Moreover, with major telescopes now on all the continents, the coverage for this appearance of Halley's will be more comprehensive. Many of today's amateur astronomers, who will fill in many of the observing gaps between big telescopes, are equipped with instruments that are as good as or better than most of the professional telescopes of 1910. Being able to deploy instruments on spacecraft orbiting high above the distorting atmosphere, and to within a few thousand miles of the comet's nucleus, should be of incalculable value in learning the true nature of comets.

The capability of today's telescopes is not measured alone in their number and distribution or the size and fine polish of their mirrors. In recent years the technology of astronomy has advanced considerably through esoteric adaptations of modern electronics and no single advance is considered more significant than the invention of the electronic detector that made it possible for Palomar to see Halley's Comet when it was still so far away. This detector, called a charge-coupled device, or CCD, is a rectangular silicon chip that is smaller than a postage stamp and not much thicker than a piece of photographic film. Some versions of the CCD chip contain an array of 250,000 individual microscopic light-sensitive elements, 500 lines of 500 picture elements (pixels) each. When a photon captured by a telescope's mirror hits one of these elements, the energy creates a free electron. An astronomer, Bradford

A. Smith of the University of Arizona, once explained it this way: "Think of it as an array of little buckets. Five hundred by 500 little buckets sitting there in the silicon, and each bucket, each pixel, will collect some number of electrons in proportion to the light falling on it." The electrons in the many picture elements are read out sequentially to form a picture. And little of the light falling escapes detection by these devices; their efficiency in collecting incoming light is as much as 80 to 90 percent, compared to the 20 percent efficiency of many cameras. These devices, in short, do not miss much. The CCD, said Donald K. Yeomans of the Jet Propulsion Laboratory, is "the giant step forward."

So it was that astronomers were able to spot Halley's Comet in October 1982 when it was three times farther away from the Sun than at its first sighting in 1909 and about 2,000 times fainter. This, astronomers say, is a rough measure of how far astronomy has come in seven decades and how much more revealing the observations of Halley's Comet should be this time.

The world's astronomers are now not only better equipped but better organized. They have gone to great lengths to avoid the troubles and scientific disappointments of 1910. The result is the establishment of a cooperative effort known as the International Halley Watch.

This organization began to take shape in the minds of scientists at the Jet Propulsion Laboratory in the summer of 1979. Much attention had been devoted already to various possible space missions to the comet, but comparatively little thought had been given to coordinated ground-based observations. By some of these observations the spacecraft would be guided to their destinations. But ground-based observations would be the only means by which scientists could hope to create a picture of the comet in its many guises, from being nothing more

(Opposite) Donald K. Yeomans of the Jet Propulsion Laboratory.
(Left) Zdenek Sekanina of JPL is on the team studying the comet's nucleus.
(Below) Stephen Edberg of International Halley Watch.

than a ball of ice to a dynamic object of glowing gases and streaming dust. The technology was available. It was possible to observe the comet almost continuously during the months of its journey through the inner Solar System and from those observations to produce what would be in effect a motion picture of this once-in-a-lifetime astronomical event. It was possible, but not inevitable.

Prior to Halley's 1910 visit, scientists had also established an observing network and a central committee to serve as a clearinghouse for data. The effort fell short of its intended goals, however, because many observatories did not cooperate with the central committee. Their sightings were sporadic. Their data were often not shared; much of the 1910 work was never published. It was not a performance today's scientists wanted to repeat, for it would be such a waste of their time and exceptional technologies to be haphazard in the way they greeted this illustrious visitor.

Under the leadership of Louis Friedman of JPL, a group of American scientists identified the general ground-based scientific goals and recommended the kind of organization that might meet them. Teams of astronomers should be established according to the many different techniques used to observe the comet. Each team would be headed by scientists prominent in that particular discipline, who would determine the standards for observing the comet and forms in which the data should be reported. It was decided, too, that the organization must be international, because the observations had to be worldwide to be most productive. The concept was discussed at scientific conferences in 1980 and 1981

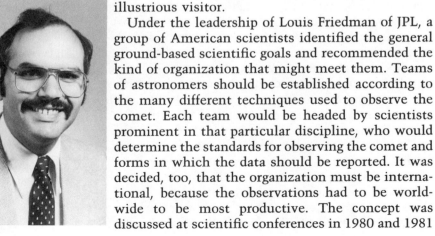

and finally became a reality as the International Halley Watch.

Leadership of the Halley Watch was centered at two places—the Jet Propulsion Laboratory in Pasadena, California, for the Western Hemisphere and the Remeis Observatory of the University of Erlangen-Nürnberg in Bamberg, West Germany, for the Eastern Hemisphere. Ray Newburn headed the Pasadena center, and Jurgen Rahe headed the Bamberg center. The United States, through the National Aeronautics and Space Administration, supported the Pasadena operation. West Germany supported the Bamberg operation. Ground-based observations were organized around seven disciplines, and by 1984 almost 1,000 scientists from some fifty countries had become involved. The individual scientists, in most cases, had to arrange for their own financial support.

The scope of their planned efforts can be seen in the Halley Watch's seven observational disciplines. They are as follows:

**Large-scale Phenomena.** A worldwide network of observatories was set to use wide-angle photography to study the comet's tail and its interaction with the solar wind. The goal is to obtain wide-angle images at approximately one-hour intervals for extended periods during the prime observing periods from Earth, roughly November–December 1985 and March–April 1986. Only with such frequency of observation will it be possible to examine the highly variable tail. As the astronomer E. E. Barnard said in 1908, discussing another comet, the great changes in the tail were much too rapid to follow from photographs taken on successive nights at one observatory. Greater coverage was necessary, he said, "to give a complete history of the transformation of some of these masses throughout their visible existence." Much of the work will be done with Schmidt telescopic cameras, which have a typical field of view of 5 to 10 degrees. The team is headed by John C. Brandt and M. B. Niedner of the Goddard Space Flight Center in Greenbelt, Maryland, and Jurgen Rahe of Bamberg.

**Near-nucleus Studies.** With high-resolution photographic and electronic imaging, including the CCD, scientists hope to gather data on the rotation rate, surface structure, thermophysical properties, and general activity of Halley's nucleus. The nucleus is believed to be structurally nonhomogeneous, which would account for the varying patterns of the dust and plasma structures near the nucleus, particularly the jets of matter that have a way of affecting the comet's course. Because these features can vary from day to day, sometimes within hours, relatively continuous coverage will be needed from observatories round the world. Leaders of this team are Stephen M. Larson of the University of Arizona, Zdenek Sekanina of JPL, and Rahe.

**Photometry and Polarimetry.** The objective of these observations is to determine the abundances and distribution of gas and dust in the comet's coma and to infer from that the chemical composition of the nucleus. The primary instrument is normally a photomultiplier tube, a kind of light meter that is attached to telescopes. By viewing the incoming light through different filters, the meters should be able to determine some of the different molecules boiling off the comet as it is heated by its passage close to the Sun. Polarimetry with polarizing filters or prisms should determine the size of dust grains in the coma and changes in the nature of the particles released. When Halley's is still far away and faint, from late 1984 through late 1985 and from the summer of 1986 to the summer of 1987, the photometric work would be done with a few large telescopes. At the comet's closest approaches, a larger number of relatively small telescopes would join the effort. The team is led by M. F. A'Hearn of the University of Maryland and V. Vanysek of Charles University in Prague.

**Radio Science.** One of the major technologies developed since Halley's 1910 visit, radio astronomy should yield valuable data on the chemical composition of the coma, nucleus, and tail. This should help to confirm the importance of water as a major constituent of comets and to identify other molecules as well. From the energy emitted by the comet in the radio wavelengths and detected by antennas on Earth, scientists expect to study the nature of the parent molecules subliming from the nucleus into the coma, the chemical processes in the coma itself, and the production and dispersal of molecular ions into the tail. Analysis of these data, moreover, could provide fundamental information on the conditions under which comets were formed and thus on the conditions when the Solar System was young. In addition, attempts will be made to bounce radar signals off the comet's nucleus, an exceedingly difficult task, to obtain information on the size, surface structure, and rotation of the nucleus. Scientists caution that the radar experiments may not succeed unless Halley's nucleus is large enough—at least 2 to 3 miles in diameter—to serve as a target for the radar signals. Leaders of this team are W. M. Irvine and F. P. Schloerb of the University of Massachusetts, F. Gérard of Meudon Observatory in France, and R. D. Brown and P. Godfrey of Monash University in Australia.

**Spectroscopy and Spectrophotometry.** This is yet another means by which scientists plan to extract chemical information out of the visible light coming from Halley's Comet. One of astronomy's standard analytical techniques, spectroscopy involves dissecting the light through diffraction gratings and prisms and capturing the spectral signatures on photographic plates or electronic devices like CCDs. Observations began in late 1983 when the comet was still far away. But the first results were not obtained until February and March of 1984. Astronomers at Kitt Peak, using a 158-inch telescope outfitted with a CCD, made spectroscopic observations suggesting that the comet's surface is very red in color, indicating that the icy nucleus may be covered with a kind of primeval material rich in complex organic carbon-bearing molecules similar to materials found in coal tar and certain primitive meteorites. According to the team leaders, the objectives are (1) to observe the comet over as large a range of distances as possible, (2) to identify new chemical substances in and around the comet, (3) to monitor production rates and densities of various chemical substances, (4) to determine abundances of as many species as possible, (5) to measure various molecules, atoms, and ions, and (6) to map the velocity of the expanding coma and plasma tail. The leaders are Susan Wyckoff and Peter Wehinger of Arizona State University and Michele Festou of the French Space Agency.

**Infrared Spectroscopy and Radiometry.** Infrared observations have already been tested in detecting the thermal emissions from several comets in the 1970s. This led to the identification of silicate dust in comets Bennett and Kohoutek. But the technology has improved vastly since then, and Halley's should provide a better target. So scientists believe that their infrared measurements this time should lead to important discoveries about cometary gases and dust. They expect to be able to make direct observations of cometary ices, which until now have been only inferred indirectly. Indeed, the team leaders, Roger

Knacke of the State University of New York at
Stony Brook and T. Encrenaz of the Paris Observatory, believe that infrared observations by astronomers around the world will contribute to all of the
Halley Watch objectives, which are to characterize
the structure, basic physical processes, and chemical
nature of cometary nuclei, atmospheres, and tails.

**Astrometry.** Astrometric observations, studies of
Halley's position in relation to stars, began the moment the comet was first sighted by Palomar in
1982. By seeing where the comet is at several points
along its course and plotting from that its predicted
orbit, scientists are able to calculate where the
comet should be at any particular time during its
journey through the inner Solar System. Because a
comet is a dynamic thing, sometimes changing
shape and velocity in a matter of hours, speed is essential in this area of Halley Watch observations.
Astronomers were primed to rush their astrometric
data to the Pasadena office by telephone, telex, or
computer-to-computer transmissions; the same
communications links were available to other scientists who had data to share with their colleagues in
the Watch, though the pressure to be swift was not
as great on them. From these reports of Halley sightings, Donald Yeomans, an astrometry team leader,
would make regular calculations to predict "within
a gnat's eyelash" where the comet will be at any
given time. (Other team leaders are Richard M. West
of the European Southern Observatory, Brian G.
Marsden of the Smithsonian Astrophysical Observatory, and Robert S. Harrington of the United States
Naval Observatory.) This is important to all astronomers who'll be searching the skies to make their various observations of Halley's. The observations,
furthermore, would help determine what effect
gases streaming from the icy nucleus have on the
comet's velocity; such nongravitational perturba-

tions are believed to account for the slight errors in predictions of when comets return to the inner Solar System.

Predictions of Halley's course, precise and up-to-date, would become increasingly critical as the spacecraft of the Soviet Union, the European Space Agency, and Japan prepared for their cometary encounters in March 1986. But it was essential that the entire operation of the International Halley Watch be functioning smoothly. To see if everything was ready there was a dress rehearsal of sorts in March 1984.

After sundown every day for a week astronomers in many countries, professionals and amateurs, peered into the southwestern sky for a glimpse of a fuzzy patch of light 74 million miles away. This was the Comet Crommelin, small and faint, no Halley's by any measure but a suitable object for practice observations. It was passing Earth at about the same distance and same position as would Halley's in March 1986. The astronomers, wherever they were, made their observations, tabulated the results, and fed the data to either Pasadena or Bamberg. All this was reviewed with an eye to seeing if scientists were following standardized methods of observation and data reporting and if there were any important gaps in the networks. Amateurs were especially encouraged to practice on Crommelin and other comets so that they would be ready for the main event. The week-long Crommelin rehearsal, said Newburn of JPL, "allows us to flex all our muscles and see if we have muscles, or whether it's all flab."

By then, Halley's was 700 million miles away, still far beyond Jupiter. There was time to make adjustments, to change some procedures, to fill in some of the observational gaps, to recruit more team members. There was also time to prepare the computers at Pasadena to serve as an archive of all the Halley Watch information. The archive will not be a collection of interpretations or ordinary research papers, though an index to published papers might be furnished. (Scientists participating in the Halley Watch retain the right to publish their data as well as their interpretations in the usual journals.) The archive will, instead, consist of all data gathered by scientists in all the disciplines. Publication of the archive is expected to occur in 1989.

There will be many times when all the scientists and all the facilities at the disposal of the International Halley Watch will be focused on the comet in unison. These special Halley Watch Days, as they are called, are chosen to give a representative view of the comet's evolution as it streaks in toward the Sun and as it moves back out into the Solar System. At no time will the ground-based observers be more alert than after the comet emerges from behind the Sun in late February 1986. This will be the time to see the comet in its most active state. This will be the time when a greeting party of four spacecraft, if everything goes according to plan, should be closing in for a look at Halley's in a way no other comet has ever been studied. March 1986 will be a time like no other time in astronomy.

The Soviet Union, in partnership with France, has the most ambitious plans, with two spacecraft equipped with television cameras and assorted sensing instruments to make the Halley run. The two craft are called Vega 1 and Vega 2. Vega is an acronym derived from the Russian names for the missions' two targets, Venera (Venus) and Gallei (Halley).

After launching in December 1984 from the Tyuratam space center in Kazakhstan, the two Vegas were to head first to Venus, where each one was to release smaller craft to make landings on the planet and to send balloons down to study circulation patterns of the dense Venusian atmosphere. The visit to Venus had once been the missions' sole objective. But at a cocktail party in 1979, a French scientist on the project, Jacques Blamont, mentioned to the Russians that the Venus craft could easily be redirected to rendezvous with Halley's Comet. "Suddenly all hell broke loose," Blamont recalled, and in a few months the Soviet Union had its sights set on the comet.

When the two Vegas fly by Venus in June 1985, if all goes well, the planet's gravity will give them a boost of energy and a change of course, sending them out toward where Halley's would be in March 1986. Halley Watch scientists will be supplying the Soviet navigators with updates on the comet's course so that last-minute corrections can be made in aiming the Vegas to their target. The plan is for Vega 1 to pass through the comet's atmosphere, to within 6,000 miles of its core, on March 6, 1986. Vega 2 would follow three days later and risk an even closer approach of about 2,000 miles to the nucleus.

Whether the Vegas survive their brush with the comet is problematical. The crafts' communications systems and other critical parts are only shielded against impacts of high-velocity fine particles. The Vegas should transmit pictures and considerable data as they fly into the comet, and scientists can hardly wait. For the Vegas are expected to gather data on the size, shape, surface properties, and temperatures of the comet's nucleus. They will examine the atmosphere surrounding the nucleus, sampling the gas and dust to measure its composition. They should be able to characterize the chemical reactions and physical processes in the coma and study gas and particle composition at various distances along the tail of the comet. The Vegas should also observe the interactions between the comet and the solar wind.

To accomplish these objectives, each of the Vegas carries an identical payload of scientific instruments. These include two black-and-white television cameras, one narrow angle (1,200-mm focal length) and one wide angle (200-mm focal length). The television system, developed by a team of Soviet, French, and Hungarian engineers, contains charge-coupled devices (CCDs) to achieve even greater detail. At the closest approach and under the best conditions, the cameras should be able to photograph any features of the comet's nucleus that are larger than 180 feet. No ground-based instruments have ever probed a comet's nucleus. Other instruments on board are spectrometers to examine the chemistry of the coma, an infrared spectrometer to determine the size and temperatures of the nucleus and dust particles in the coma, and a magnetometer to measure magnetic fields involved in the solar wind-comet interaction. Comet dust will be studied by several instruments, such as a dust-plasma counter to measure minute particles, an acoustic dust counter consisting of a metal plate to count particle impacts, and a mass spectrometer to get the mass and chemical composition of dust in the coma. In addition, instruments will assess the masses, energies, and wave phenomena in the plasmas and neutral gases of the coma.

According to American scientists, Soviet officials have promised to release a complete set of the Vega results within two years after the encounter and to provide "quick-look" images almost immediately so that other scientists can perhaps adjust some of their observing tactics or refine the interpretations of their own data. Soviet officials have not usually been so forthcoming in sharing the results of their space missions. Moreover, the Soviets have agreed to hand over immediately tracking data from the Vegas that should help the European Space Agency improve the targeting accuracy for its Halley probe, the Giotto spacecraft.

Arrangements for this cooperative approach to tracking the Halley probes were concluded at a sci-

**The Giotto spacecraft, the star of the European Space Agency's effort, is equipped to perform ten experiments. (ESA)**

entific conference in Tokyo in December 1983. The United States, though it has no Halley spacecraft of its own, agreed to use its deep-space tracking antennas to help both the Soviet and European missions. "If it works," said Don Yeomans of JPL, "it will be quite an exercise in international cooperation."

Going to Halley's represents the Europeans' debut in interplanetary exploration. Through their joint enterprise, the eleven-nation European Space Agency, they built the sophisticated Giotto spacecraft. The plan calls for launching the spacecraft with the Ariane rocket from Kourou in French Guiana in July 1985. The South American launching base, situated in the Atlantic Ocean near the Equator and the infamous Devil's Island, has become Europe's Cape Canaveral.

"If things work out the way we hope," said David Dale, a British physicist who is the project manager, "Giotto will provide Earth's closest link with the comet."

With the help of American and Soviet tracking facilities, as well as their own, the Europeans intend to aim Giotto to a point in distant space, the "node" where the orbit of Halley's intersects the plane in which the Earth orbits. This is the point where Giotto, with a minimum of energy, should intercept Halley's trajectory on the night of March 13–14, 1986. On instructions from a control center in Darmstadt, West Germany, the craft will plunge into the comet's atmosphere at a speed of 42 miles a second. Most of the scientific instruments will begin sending data about four hours prior to closest encounter. The craft is expected to pass within some 300 miles to the Sunward side of the cometary core —dangerously close, perhaps fatally close. A sandblasting of cometary dust is likely to destroy the craft near closest approach. The European strategy, according to Rüdeger Reinhard, the project scientist, is, "Get in as close as possible, immediately relay all data to Earth in real time, and find out as much as we can before our probe dies."

In the brief time that Giotto has to examine Halley's Comet, scientists hope that it can supply them with knowledge of the composition of the coma, the physical processes and chemical reactions in both the comet's atmosphere and ionosphere, the composition of dust particles and the ratio of dust to gas, and the flow of ionized gas in the vicinity of the comet and its reaction to the solar wind.

Like the Soviet probes, Giotto will attempt to photograph the comet's nucleus to determine its size, mass, and rotational characteristics. Photography is to begin about 10 minutes before closest en-

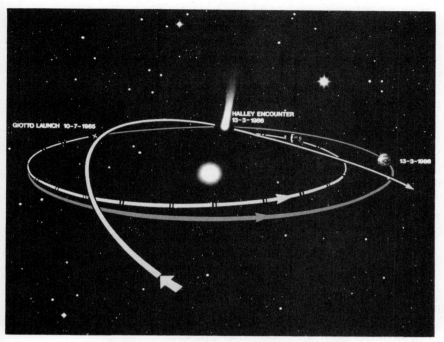

**Giotto's planned encounter with the comet.** *(ESA)*

counter, when the craft is still about 20,000 miles away but moving in fast. The system employs two television cameras, which should be able to resolve surface features as small as 100 feet. The camera system will view the comet through a mirror that turns the light 90 degrees so that the camera does not have to face directly into the dust cloud and thus risk premature damage. As Giotto moves into and away from the comet, the camera's line of sight can be swiveled 180 degrees so that it will be able to keep the comet in view during the encounter and even afterward, if the spacecraft survives.

European scientists expect their spacecraft to encounter dust bombardment beginning about one hour prior to closest approach. A thin shield of aluminum, backed by a thicker sheet of Kevlar, a material used in bulletproof vests, should afford the craft sufficient protection until the last few hundred miles. Then the bombardment of dust could cause several problems other than simple punctures. The impacting dust particles could become electrically charged and cause a plasma cloud to form in front of the craft and thus confuse the plasma experiments. Heavier dust particles could strike with enough force to cause the craft to wobble, and such a change in its orientation could result in its losing its communications link with Earth. By the time the craft was steadied, it would probably have already passed by the comet's core.

As Giotto approaches Halley's, beginning about four hours prior to closest encounter, all its sensors will be operating at one time or another, some of them functioning all the way in. There will be the photopolarimeter, measuring the polarization of light reflected from cometary dust particles in order to determine their sizes and other properties. The magnetometer, identical to the ones carried by the Voyagers that explored the outer planets, will measure the comet's magnetic field. Three small telescopes, linked to solid-state detectors, will observe dust particles as they are accelerated by solar wind. Three mass spectrometers will measure the masses of neutral gas molecules, plasma ions, and dust particles. Other sensors will determine the energies, velocities, directions of travel, and masses of charged particles in the comet's vicinity. Three microphones mounted on the craft's dust shield will detect and analyze the impacts of large particles by the vibrations they create in the shield.

Japan is also mounting a mission to Halley's. Its spacecraft is called Planet A, and as the name suggests, it marks Japan's entry into interplanetary spaceflight.

After launching a test vehicle in early 1985, to check out the performance of the rocket and the deep-space communications network, Japan plans to dispatch Planet A in August 1985 from its Kagoshima Space Center. Unlike most interplanetary probes, Planet A will be boosted directly into its intercept orbit, instead of first going into a parking orbit around the Earth. This "direct injection" method saves fuel, but at a sacrifice in flexibility. There will be no way to compensate for any errors in its aim on the comet. For that reason the Japanese will make no attempt to get very close to Halley's; their craft will probably come no closer than 60,000 miles to the comet's nucleus. Its encounter with Halley's should occur March 13, 1986, about the same time Giotto is passing by at closer range.

Even at its great distance Planet A, with its set of instruments, should return data that in many ways complement the Soviet and European missions'. Its goals are to observe the coma's growth and decay, the expanding hydrogen cloud around the nucleus, and the shock front where the solar wind meets the coma.

To carry out these investigations Planet A, a cylindrical craft, is outfitted with only two scientific instruments, an ultraviolet camera and a solar-wind analyzer. The camera consists of an ultraviolet telescope and that invaluable tool, a charge-coupled device (CCD). Its field of view is 2.5 degrees and its resolution no better than 20 miles at a range of 60,000 miles, which means Planet A will not be seeing Halley's nucleus. Instead, it will concentrate on images of the cloud of atomic hydrogen, glowing in ultraviolet, that extends for tens of thousands of miles out from the comet. This cloud is invisible to ground-based observers because Earth's atmosphere absorbs nearly all ultraviolet radiation. The second experiment, a solar-wind analyzer similar to a photomultiplier, will measure the distribution and direction of solar wind in the vicinity of Halley's.

It will be a busy few days, those days in March 1986 when four spacecraft visit Halley's and send back the first close-up images of a comet. From the ground astronomers will be looking through telescopes to see from afar what the spacecraft are seeing up close. They will be providing the big-picture context into which the details of the spacecraft data must be fitted. High-altitude aircraft will also be going aloft then with telescopes and other means of studying the comet.

It will be a busy time in space for the Soviet Union, the European Space Agency, and Japan. But what of the United States? With the American record for success in interplanetary flight, the landings on Mars, and the spectacular flybys of Jupiter and Saturn, one would have expected to see an American spacecraft out there with the greeting party. But there will be none, a fact that still upsets and saddens many American planetary scientists. Stephen J. Edberg, a JPL astronomer with the International Halley Watch, lamented: "I'm still crying about not having an American mission."

American scientists will not be altogether grounded, however. The Giotto scientific teams include thirty-one Americans. A space shuttle will go into orbit in March 1986 carrying three ultraviolet telescopes to study Halley's from afar while the other spacecraft are up close. The Solar Maximum Mission satellite, familiarly known as Solar Max, which was repaired by space-walking astronauts in April 1984, is set to observe Halley's when the comet is especially close to the Sun and thus not easily seen by other telescopic instruments. Another American spacecraft, which had been examining various physical properties of interplanetary space, was rerouted in 1983 to encounter the tail of another comet, Giacobini-Zinner, in September 1985. It will not be able to examine the comet in the detail scientists might desire, but it will be the world's first close-up inspection of a comet—some consolation to the Americans who had fought hard but in vain to have a Halley's Comet mission.

As the various spacecraft arrive in the vicinity of Halley's, there will undoubtedly be those who will pause and think of what might have been. For a few years in the late 1970s, American Solar System scientists and spacecraft designers made several proposals for ambitious missions to Halley's, including ones that would have had a craft fly in formation with the comet for prolonged observations. The idea of flying to Halley's Comet seemed irresistible, the actual concepts seemed technologically sound, and the promise of scientific reward seemed compelling. But the National Aeronautics and Space Administration at the time was in the depths of a depression: Its annual budgets had been pared to the bone, and nearly all of its available money was committed to completing the troubled development of the space shuttle project. None of the proposals for a Halley mission ever won financial approval. Then it was too late to mount a mission.

What might have been, if a 1977 proposal had been adopted, would have been something to behold—a craft sailing to Halley's, scudding through space with the "breeze" from the light of the Sun— sunbeams and nothing more. Photons of sunlight have no mass but they do have momentum. They exert a pervasive pressure that can push against gossamer sails in the vacuum of space. Analysis by engineers at the Jet Propulsion Laboratory found that solar sailing—deploying a vast plastic mainsail or an array of plastic blades like helicopter blades—was not only feasible but preferable for long-duration flights. The thrust developed by a solar sail is small, but unlike fuel-limited chemical propulsion systems, the sail would provide thrust continually throughout a trip, for years on end, building up velocity until a craft might attain speeds of up to 124,000 miles an hour. The JPL engineers proposed launching such a craft in the early 1980s, directing it to a rendezvous with Halley's, and letting it sail in formation within a few miles of the comet for several months. No one bought the idea for a Halley mission; the concept was deemed too speculative.

An alternative concept, going to Halley's by ion drive, was considered for a while and then abandoned. Some engineering models of ion engines had already been tested in spaceflight. They run on sunlight collected by solar panels and converted to electricity, which is used to charge electrically, or ionize, mercury vapor. The charged mercury gas is concentrated and expelled in a steady, flameless, violet exhaust—ion drive. Since a small tank of mercury would be sufficient for years of flight, a spacecraft operating on ion drive could be sent on the long journey to Halley's, observe it for several days, and then fly on to rendezvous with another comet, Tempel 2, for comparative studies. Although the ion-drive technology seemed ready, NASA finally rejected the idea.

Halley advocates within NASA lowered their sights and, in their final proposal, called for a rather straightforward intercept flight. A spacecraft, deployed from the space shuttle, would cross the orbit of Halley's for a brief inspection. Many of its scientific instruments would be similar to those being planned for the European and Soviet missions. But American engineers, with some justification, argued that their craft would have superior navigation and imaging systems along the lines of the highly successful Voyagers that flew to the outer planets. This proposal, like the others, found no support in Washington. By 1982, it became clear that there would be no American mission to Halley's Comet.

The one American space mission dedicated specifically to Halley observations will be flown by a space shuttle in March 1986. The mission, called Astro I, will employ an assemblage of telescopes that were designed to study distant stars and galaxies in the ultraviolet wavelengths. When it became clear that the instruments would be ready in time for Halley's visit, NASA scientists decided to devote the first Astro flight to the comet, not to the stars.

The three main instruments are ultraviolet telescopes designed to operate in low-Earth orbit and make simultaneous observations of the comet with three different objectives in mind. One telescope, developed by a scientific team from Johns Hopkins University, will make brightness observations in the far ultraviolet. Aside from revealing something of the comet's chemical composition, it should give scientists their first measure of a comet's helium abundance. A telescope designed by University of Wisconsin scientists will provide spectroscopic and polarization measurements of the comet and perhaps some insights into the formation and destruction of dust grains in a comet's tail. The third telescope, developed by scientists at the Goddard Space Flight Center, is an imaging system aimed at determining the overall cometary structure and observing how the close encounter with the Sun boils off material from the nucleus and thus affects the comet's structure. Two cameras will be added to the Astro instrument package specifically for the Halley observations. The instruments, being assembled under the direction of the Marshall Space Flight Center in Huntsville, Alabama, will ride in the shuttle's cargo bay.

Although it tends to be eclipsed by the Halley preparations, another American mission to another comet, Giacobini-Zinner, will give scientists their first opportunity to probe a comet with a spacecraft. This is to occur on September 11, 1985, six months before the other craft reach Halley's. The mission is an example of how to take an old spacecraft that had

essentially accomplished its objectives and give it a
new lease on life, even a new name.

Before the International Sun-Earth Explorer 3 disappeared behind the Moon on December 22, 1983,
the little robot craft had spent five years observing
the flow of charged particles coming from the Sun,
the solar wind. When it emerged from behind the
Moon an hour later, the craft had a new name, International Cometary Explorer, and a new mission: to
fly close by an old and relatively small comet that
was approaching the inner Solar System. The force
of lunar gravity changed the craft's course and gave
it a boost of increased speed in the direction of
Giacobini-Zinner. This comet was discovered in
1900, and in its ten observed appearances near the
Sun since then, the comet has displayed an erratic
behavior, the apparent result of material vaporizing
from the nucleus like wildly firing jets, and a well-
developed tail of charged particles. The craft, now
known as ICE, pronounced "icy," is being aimed for
passage through that tail of particles about 9,000
miles from the core. The comet appears to be cooperative; Giacobini-Zinner was picked up by astronomers at Kitt Peak on April 3, 1984, in ample time to
begin charting and predicting its precise course.

Robert W. Farquhar, an engineer at the Goddard
Space Flight Center, conceived and plotted the re-
direction of the Explorer to a cometary target. The
idea came to him when he heard that all other proposals for an American Halley mission had been
abandoned. First, he thought of sending the Explorer
to Halley's, but the timing and distances ruled that
out. Comet experts then discovered the opportunity
to visit Giacobini-Zinner. Many scientists doubted
that the complex maneuvers devised by Farquhar—
three earlier passes by the Moon, then the final one
in December—could succeed in changing the craft's
course with sufficient precision to make the comet
run.

The Explorer does not carry photographic equipment, but several of its instruments for studying the solar wind will be able to examine the magnetic fields and electrified gases in the comet's tail. This should give scientists some basis for interpreting what is learned from the more spectacular Halley's Comet. And, besides, the mission is a bargain. Farquhar estimated that the Explorer's comet rendezvous would cost $3 million to $5 million, as against the $200 million it would have cost for a brand-new spacecraft.

Even so, it will be Halley's Comet that will command the rapt attention of astronomers and the public alike in the months to come. It will be seen from near and far, by spacecraft and by ground-based telescopes, by the human eye and by electronic sensors that no eye can match. It may not arouse the fears of yore, but it is sure to inspire wonder and to bring to those who study it well messages from long ago and faraway when the Solar System was young.

# The Apparition of 1986

After leaving the Earth's viewers in the spring of 1910, Halley's traveled out on a long lonely arc that took it farthest from the Sun in 1948, 3.2 billion miles away. Now as it heads back, it makes its closest inbound approach to the Earth, coming within 57.7 million miles of it on November 27, 1985. It then circles around behind the Sun, reaches its closest approach to it, perihelion, on February 9, 1986, emerges and makes its closest outbound approach to Earth, on April 11, 1986, when it will be 39 million miles away. By this time, its seventy-six-year journey to the outer limits and back has begun again.

It will be hidden from all view behind the Sun during its brightest, most agitated period, perihelion. It will be too low on the horizon in high northern latitudes to be plainly visible during its next most dramatic phase, the period after it has looped around the Sun, leaving many northerners to content themselves with viewing it during the earlier, less spectacular period, as the comet first makes its approach toward the Sun. Thus, for northerners, the best viewing will be in January of 1986. March and April will be the best viewing periods for those in southern latitudes.

At its brightest moments and in the best of conditions, Halley's Comet will be visible to the naked eye. But there is very little certainty about just how visible. When the comet IRAS-Araki-Alcock made its close approach to Earth, amateur observers everywhere went to their backyards and to building tops to see it. Mostly, they were disappointed in its amorphous, undramatic appearance.

Halley's, too, will proffer a host of problems to observers, although it should, in any event, be a much bigger success than IRAS-Araki-Alcock. There is nevertheless the deplorable possibility that the comet will be dim or virtually invisible from vantage points in and around the world's great cities. The world that the comet returns to, after all, is much different from the one it saw at the end of the first decade of this century. America, although already a great nation, was still largely rural. The great sprawl of Los Angeles was unimaginable. And it is just as well that no one then could have dreamed that something called the Long Island Expressway would grow into a slow-moving collection of lights merging into a single, enormous glow. Light pollution will be a great enemy of Halley's Comet this time around.

A remarkable mosaic of satellite images from the Defense Meteorological Satellite Program suggests how the light around the world is now distributed in the night sky. From this space-borne view, it is clear that the northeastern United States appears to suffer far more from the lighting than does any other part of the country or Canada, although the whole eastern third of the nation seems much brighter than the

**(Overleaf) Light pollution will be a major obstacle to viewing the comet. A mosaic of satellite images from the Defense Meteorological Satellite Program indicates the areas of the world most subject to light pollution.**

Some of the bright areas are transient, such as an aurora off Norway and fires in India and Southeast Asia.

rest. There is relative tranquillity, as these cameras capture it, in the middle of the country down through Mexico and Central and South America.

This awareness of modern light pollution inspired a movement early in the eighties to persuade the nation's cities to give us a break. One spokesman for the movement was Fred Schaaf, a columnist for *Astronomy* magazine, who founded Dark Skies for Comet Halley, with the sole intention of getting urban governments to turn down their lights for a few nights when the comet becomes most visible. Progress in this effort was being reported in the DSCH *Journal* (RD 2, Box 248, Millville, New Jersey 08332).

The hostility or friendliness of the cities aside, there are several other factors that will affect how well the comet is seen. The Moon, for instance, may play havoc with one's observations, and so observational forays should be planned with a complete awareness of the rising and setting of the Moon.

Advanced amateur astronomers with telescopes or high-powered binoculars will join the professional astronomers to begin recording the development of the tail early in the fall of 1985 as the comet approaches the orbit of Mars. These accomplished amateurs will take readings that will be used to help determine the tail's composition. For the average comet-gazing enthusiast with binoculars who gets himself away from the city, the comet will be visible in the Northern Hemisphere by early November and December of 1985. Without the interference of excessive light pollution, the comet is viewable if it is above the local horizon and if the Sun has set and has dropped 18 degrees below the horizon. (It helps the novice to visualize astronomical degrees by realizing that from one horizon to the other is 180 degrees; from the horizon to a line straight up from the point of observation is 90.)

Still, one must not expect a Columbia Pictures

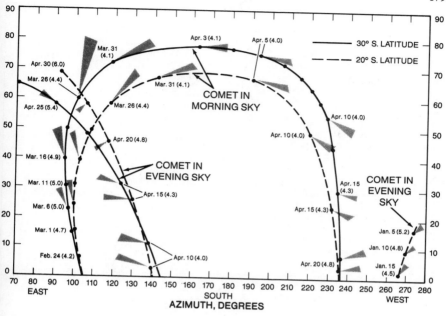

Comet Halley observing conditions in 1986 for observers located at 20° and 30° south latitudes. Comet positions are given for the beginning of morning astronomical twilight or the end of evening astronomical twilight. Approximate total visual magnitudes are given in parentheses following the dates. Viewing with binoculars and ideal observing conditions are assumed. (*Adapted from* The Comet Halley Handbook *by Donald Yeomans*)

version of night suddenly turned into high noon and a ball of flame heading for the World Trade Center. What one will see by late December and early January is a small fuzzy faint disk with a tail only a few degrees long near the horizon.

The comet will become theoretically visible to the naked eye in late December 1985, when it reaches a magnitude of 6. That means that its brightness—or rather its apparent brightness—from Earth is about the same as that of a star just visible to the naked eye. Apparent magnitude is distinguished from absolute, or intrinsic, brightness, which re-

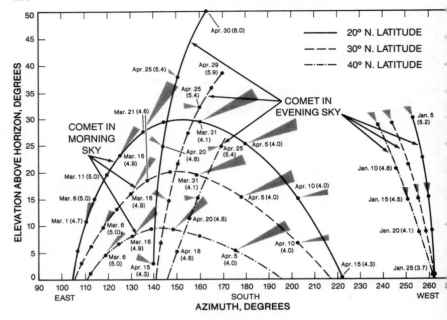

**Comet Halley observing conditions in 1986 for observers located at 20°, 30°, and 40° north latitudes. Comet positions are given for the beginning of morning astronomical twilight or the end of evening astronomical twilight. Approximate total visual magnitudes are given in parentheses following the dates. Viewing with binoculars and ideal observing conditions are assumed. (*Adapted from* The Comet Halley Handbook *by Donald Yeomans*)**

mains about the same wherever the comet is. Magnitude scale is inversely proportional to brightness —the lower the number, the greater the brightness ("a star of the 1st magnitude"). A star of magnitude 5 is 2.5 times brighter than one of magnitude 6, and one of magnitude 7 is 2.5 times fainter than one of magnitude 6.

Halley's Comet will have become visible to those with high-powered binoculars in October of 1985, when it will have reached magnitude 9.

Assuming the comet's brightness in 1910 is a good model for 1986—and astronomers make that assumption—then brightness can be calculated for every night during the 1985–86 apparition by using the 1910 figures.

Visual brightness estimates of a comet have been made by comparing it to out-of-focus stars of known brightness. Studies of Halley's in 1910 determined that it had an apparent magnitude—before it reached perihelion and before it made its closest approach to the Sun but after it had come within 316 million miles of Earth—of a relatively bright, but far from the brightest, star. After perihelion, it was far brighter, eventually reaching zero magnitude—as bright as Arcturus or Saturn near its brightest. And its tail reached an all-time record of 109 degrees, that is, it stretched slightly farther than halfway across the sky.

In the first weeks of January 1986, the comet will become more and more visible, growing steadily brighter each night and its tail growing longer and longer. With binoculars it will be observable for one or two hours after sunset in the Northern Hemisphere but for much less time in the Southern, and it will appear in a background of stars with an apparent magnitude of about 5. The visiting comet will be located in the background of stars forming the constellation Aquarius, not far from Jupiter. On January 13, it will appear with the crescent Moon, which may add another touch of beauty to an historic celestial tapestry. The added attraction of the Moon will be brief, however. As happened with Kohoutek in 1974, moonlight will now have to be redefined as natural light pollution—that is to say, the Moon's illumination will begin to interfere with the Halley observations as it increases each night and the comet begins to curve around the Sun and disappear.

Exactly how bright it will be is impossible to say, because of the comet's own unpredictable aberrations, and there is some disagreement among the experts. The amateur astronomers Charles Morris and John Bortle forecast that Halley might be as bright as

Polaris, the North Star, with a magnitude of 2.5. But
Dr. Brian Marsden of the Harvard-Smithsonian Astrophysical Observatory in Cambridge, Massachusetts, points out that the Polaris-level light from a
comet, whose light is also diffuse, would be fuzzy
and difficult to see with the unaided eye. This will
be particularly true of Halley's at locations as far
north as New York, where it will never rise much
above the horizon during the evenings when it is approaching the Sun. Later, after it has rounded the
Sun, it will be brighter, Dr. Marsden concedes. According to Bortle, "It will be more impressive than
many had been forecasting," but he too warns that it
will not be easily seen by those living in northern
cities.

Once the comet does round the Sun and is back in
sight again after its perihelion passage, Halley's
Comet will enter the predawn sky in early March in
both the Northern and Southern hemispheres. At
that time it will be bordering the Milky Way in the
neighborhoods of Sagittarius and Scorpius. It will
continue to increase in brightness, according to the
Whipple-Marsden-Sekanina-Yeomans   projections,
until it reaches its maximum apparent brightness in
early April—2.5 to 4.0. In the Southern Hemisphere
in early April it will be present in the dark night sky
for about nine hours. At a northern latitude of 30
degrees—that is Texas, Florida, the Caribbean,
northern Africa, India, southern China—there will
be nearly four hours of binocular viewing, but the
comet will be close to the horizon and the viewing
will be much better farther south. At the northern
latitude of 40 degrees—Chicago, New York, Madrid,
Tokyo, for example—viewing will not be possible
again until late April; it will continue until June 15
but by then for an average of only about an hour each
night.

***Amateurs in*** The stage was set back in 1909 for the coordinated
***the Halley*** studies that will be made of the comet during and
***Watch*** after the 1986 apparition. On September 11, 1909,
Halley's Comet was recovered photographically by
Prof. Max Wolf at Heidelberg, and two months later
the Comet Committee of the Astronomical and Astrophysical Society of America proposed worldwide,
coordinated observations. The society was swamped
with data, even though some observatories refused
to cooperate. But it had neither enough people nor
enough money to use and absorb the material. Pi-
oneering, comprehensive studies of some parts of
the data—principally the comet's 1910 perihelion
passage—were made by Nicholas T. Bobrovnikoff of
the Lick Observatory but these were not published
until 1931.

The current program, called the International Halley Watch, will be directed from the Jet Propulsion
Laboratory in Pasadena, California, and the Remeis
Observatory in West Germany. One of its goals will
be to standardize the observational techniques and
promote simultaneous viewing.

A horde of amateur observers will join the professionals in giving Comet Halley careful attention as
it makes what is sometimes described as its third
pass by the Sun in modern times—the other two
being in 1835 and 1910. The amateurs will certainly
number in the many thousands. Their large numbers will make the geographic coverage more complete, and it will lessen the overall interference of
bad weather. Moreover, amateurs will not be under
the same constraints of allotted time schedules that
are imposed on professionals, and there will be some
observations that will be easier for the amateurs to
make. Overall, the amateurs will accumulate many
more hours of observing than the professionals will.
The amateurs will be using instruments every bit as

good as those available to professional observers during the 1910 apparition—in many ways, better ones —and thus will provide data so similar to the kind accumulated earlier that the records may offer excellent points of comparison.

The key to useful amateur participation in this endeavor is, of course, the willingness to make observations in a disciplined fashion so that they qualify as true science. Visual observations (as opposed to all the "invisible" data that can be gathered) are perhaps the most straightforward and will be the most commonly made. But, common or not, visual observation is an immensely important area of science. And it will be carried out almost exclusively by amateurs. With conventional visual observations, it is possible to estimate the magnitude of the comet, its coma size, and to make studies of the tail. The data on these observations supplied by amateurs around the world will allow for comparisons not only with those of 1910 and 1835 but, in some degree, with all previous collections of records, which were, after all, largely data drawn from simple visual observation.

Amateurs will also be called upon to contribute their photographic records of Comet Halley. This body of data will be an adjunct to the extensive photo observation the professionals will be making. Amateurs will be involved in astrometry, too, which involves the precise measurement of the position of the comet with respect to background stars. Truly advanced amateurs will help out with spectroscopic observations that require special equipment, including a prism to break down the light of the comet into its component wavelengths.

The kind of data these amateurs will be expected to provide in the visual reports, to take one of the categories, would include the coma's diameter given in minutes of arc, its magnitude reported to the nearest 0.1 magnitude, as well as many other pieces of information, equally detailed and precise.

The coordinator of amateur observations for the International Watch is Stephen J. Edberg of the JPL. He has put together a book for advanced amateurs who wish to take part in the Halley Watch effort called *International Halley Watch Amateur Observers' Manual for Scientific Studies*, a publication of Sky Publishing Corporation (49 Bay State Road, Cambridge, Massachusetts 02138-1290). Amateur observers who plan to take part in the Watch will be asked to fill out and send in Halley Watch forms on which they state their level of observational experience and whether they are novice, moderately skilled, or expert in the fields of general astronomy, in comet observing, or in meteor observing. They'll also state whether they will be taking part in visual observations, photography, astrometry, spectroscopic observations, photoelectric photometry or meteor studies, the longitude, latitude, and altitude of their regular observation site or sites, the type and power of telescopic devices or cameras being used, and whether they are planning to travel to the Southern Hemisphere for the best viewing in March or April of 1986. The contributions of the amateurs will be submitted to official recorders, whose names and addresses will be published in the *IHW Amateur Observer's Bulletin*. The recorders will judge the quality and completeness of the contributions and in turn submit them to the International Halley Watch.

It is possible, of course, to be serious about the comet without being all that serious. Which is to say it is possible to be a diligent observer of the comet purely for one's own enjoyment, the way baseball fans keep score to give them a more personal involvement in the game than they might otherwise have. The JPL manual also should be useful to those who have that semiserious inclination.

Naturally, Halley's Comet will offer a few opportunities for parting with money, some of them pretty amusing. Among the more ambitious is the Halley's Comet Society, which was founded in England but soon took on an international membership—former Prime Minister Harold Wilson and American singles tennis champion (1937–38) Don Budge are among the members. It plans to hire a 707 to fly to an island in the Indian Ocean in the spring of 1986. "We may well fill up two jets," says Brian Harpur, a former newspaperman who founded the society. Then there are the water-borne tours. Among them, Sun Line Cruises of New York announced plans early in 1984 to fly passengers from the United States to a waiting ship that will take them up the Amazon in Brazil and to begin another voyage in San Juan, Puerto Rico, sail the Caribbean, and finally cruise up the Orinoco River in Venezuela. "Many of the world's leading authorities will be on board to lecture on the history and science of comets," the cruise line said.

*The Commercial Touch*

The operators of ocean liners were not the only ones to notice the business or fund-raising possibilities of the comet. Three years before the comet's arrival, Halley's T-shirts were on the market along with Halley's models, Halley's buttons, Halley's bumper stickers, and Halley's Comet pills. The pills are offered in a different spirit from those hawked in 1910 as protection against the poison cyanogen gas from the tail of the comet that was feared to be sweeping the Earth in 1910. The 1986 pills, sold by the Grand Rapids, Michigan, Public Museum to raise money, are yogurt-covered sunflower seeds, and they contain a consumer-protection warning on the label: "Museum Surgeon General has determined that worrying about comets can be hazardous to your health." Clearly, these pills do not even pretend to be able to ward off the flu, which distinguished British astronomer Fred Hoyle insists can be

caused by invisible gaseous clouds left behind by
Comet Halley. Professor Hoyle, one hastens to add,
is pretty much alone in this theory. Clearly, too, for
almost everyone else, the comet commands a good
deal less of that awesome respect it once did. The
irreverence is evidenced not only in the pill labels
but also in such bumper stickers as "REPENT! HAL-
LEY'S IS COMING!" or "HALLEY'S COMET WATCHERS
DO IT EVERY 75 YEARS!"

One of the prime movers, along with Brian Harpur, in drumming up and organizing interest in the
1986 apparition has been Prof. Joseph M. Laufter, a
dean at Burlington County Community College in
Pemberton, New Jersey. He became involved because he was disturbed by what he perceived as the
last-minute planning and poor results for the American bicentennial celebration. So ten years before
the comet's return, he began reading and photocopy-
ing everything he could find about Halley's Comet.
In 1981 he registered an organization, Halley's
Comet Watch '86, in his name and began to publish
a newsletter. He made Halley's calendars, sold Halley's Comet wooden nickels three for a dollar,
taught an evening course on the comet, made slides,
had a Halley's medal cast, and began lobbying the
Postal Service for an official United States com-
memorative Halley's Comet stamp. He also recorded about thirty one-minute vignettes about the
comet that he plans to sell to radio stations during
the apparition. His 8- by 8-foot Halley's office is
loaded with charts, telescopes, posters, lecture
notes, and an odd assortment of papers, including
some of seven to twenty letters he receives a day
from comet fans.

"The beautiful thing is that we have found that
we all can work together," Professor Laufter said of
his fellow Halley's fanatics. "There are at least a
thousand people known to be actively interested,
some for fun, some for profit, and some out of sin-

cere respect for science and the educational value.
And it really seems as though nobody is trying to rip
anybody off." He said he himself has invested very
little money, that he is not out to make a profit, and
he will be satisfied to break even. Brian Harpur, who
does profess a certain entrepreneurial and merchan-
dising flair, has copyrighted a Halley's 1986 logo and
suggests that it will go nicely on ashtrays, cups,
saucers, tankards, and ballpoint pens. Most of the
money will go to charity, he says, though he would
not be averse to setting a little aside "for my old
age."

Others are tending more strictly to business. David Eagle (3759 76th Street, S.W., Byron Center,
Michigan 49315) has written a BASIC computer program that will direct the user where and when to
look for the comet from anywhere in the world. And
the language of the Sun Line Cruises announcement
is first-class, down-to-business salesmanship: "The
1980's will be remembered as the Halley's decade
and its appearance will be the event of a lifetime.
Unless one makes preparations to be in the right
place at the right time, [he] will miss this once-in-a-
lifetime opportunity, for Halley's comet will not return again until 2061."

# N I N E

# What Kind of Equipment?

***The Aided Eye***  One telescope manufacturer has cleverly called its new product the Comet Catcher. But when the path of a comet is well known, as is the case with Halley's, catching the comet is no big deal. Comets do not streak across the sky, like meteors, although their tails may suggest great speed. Actually they just sort of sit there, with movement difficult to discern in even an hour or two of careful observation. To "catch" the comet one merely needs to know where it is and attempt to view it under conditions that are reasonably favorable. But there will be many frustrations to deal with as the comet comes and goes this time, especially for viewers in northern latitudes, and even the most amateur of amateurs is well advised to pick up some expertise.

Before worrying about the best equipment to buy for viewing the comet, it's a good idea to know a little about the equipment you were born with. The naked eye is actually a very adaptable instrument. An important principle to understand is that of visual adaptation to the dark. Don't expect anything approaching good vision in the dark until at least 10

One company, Celestron, has produced a telescope called a
Comet Catcher; it is part of a family of telescopes—the rich
field group—that supply a bright image of a wide portion of
the sky. A rich field telescope with low magnification is
perfect for most comet-watching.

minutes have gone by. (Inexperienced amateurs constantly make the mistake of trying to see in some
meaningful way after just a few minutes in the dark;
they actually see little, become discouraged, and
give up the effort.) Experts generally suggest that 20
to 30 minutes in the dark is necessary for adequate
adaptation. To get around in the dark while your
eyes are adjusting, use a red-filtered flashlight,
which will not affect the process of adaptation. Stephen Edberg of the JPL, coordinator of amateur observations for IHW, notes that the eyes just keep
getting better as time goes on in the dark. There is
some improvement even after one to two hours. Not
only does Edberg recommend that astronomers

abandon any attempt to return to lighted areas while their eyes are growing accustomed to the dark, he goes so far as to suggest that one avoid the Sun and fluorescent light during the day. A good pair of sunglasses is the prescription here.

There is no great mystery to this remarkable ability of the human eye to get better and better in the dark. The eye responds by washing the retina, where images are formed, with something known as visual purple. That substance has the effect of making the nerve endings in the eye far more sensitive than they are in daylight. But it acts slowly. If extraneous lights, such as those in the street, are troublesome, many astronomers recommend that you can cover your head with a blanket while observing the heavens through some instrument to keep the eyes at their most sensitive. And if you need to be especially sensitive to the dark on a given night, do not look at the full Moon through binoculars or a telescope; if you do, you'll be back to square one.

**The Best Binoculars** There is almost no doubt at all that anyone who wants to make the most of watching Halley's in 1986 ought to purchase or borrow some optical assistance in the form of binoculars or a telescope. This is especially true in areas that will not oblige with the darkest and the clearest skies. The role of these lenses and mirrors is to magnify (although that is not as significant an ability with a large object like a comet as it is in viewing other celestial bodies), to make the object brighter, and to give it greater sharpness against the surrounding sky. So the correct kind of optical equipment may make the difference between seeing a distinct, recognizable comet and seeing merely an amorphous blur. It may make the tail visible when the naked eye would be searching to find it in vain. It should even make it possible to watch the tail in all its fascinating transformations, as the kinks move through it or as it disengages from the cometary head. What kind of equipment is best for this particular comet on this particular voyage? There are a great many considerations.

When you ask people who know about the night sky, the nature of comets, and the value of optical equipment what their first choice would be for observing Halley's Comet most efficiently, their answers are almost universally the same: the best pair of binoculars you can find that are specially designed to observe the likes of comets. Why so sure? For one thing binoculars have emerged in the last two or three decades as serious astronomical instruments. The astronomer and author James Muirden *(Astronomy with Binoculars)* writes that binoculars entered a new era at a single moment in 1967 when G. E. D. Alcock, the incredible British amateur, discovered an exploding star, a nova, using binoculars. Muirden says that a surge of excitement followed Alcock's discovery as amateurs took up their binoculars and began scanning the skies for another class of stars that seemed especially appropriate for this equipment: stars that fall into a kind of limbo, the so-called variable stars that are too faint for naked-eye observation and too bright for the powerful astronomical telescopes. The Binocular Sky Society in Britain was soon turning in 20,000 observations of these stars every year.

A factor of considerable relevance to purchasers of any equipment to enhance the experience of Halley's Comet, too, is that when the comet is gone, you may no longer have much interest in the sky beyond admiring it in all its naked-eye splendor. Binoculars—as opposed to a telescope—can continue their usefulness long after the once-in-a-lifetime moment of sky watching has passed.

Then there is the matter of money. Magnificent binocular instruments can still be purchased for from $200 to $400. Modest binoculars that will cer-

A good pair of 7 x 50 binoculars will serve well to gather cometary light in the night sky and supply some magnification but not so much that only a small segment of the comet can be seen.

tainly enhance the view of the comet can be found for well under $100. One is hard put to find a good telescope that can compete with those prices.

Binoculars are almost invariably portable. There's a lot to be said for that quality since so many of us will be leaving homes near urban settings and heading off into the dark reaches of the night sky to see the comet best.

Depending upon the binoculars purchased, the instrument can deliver well on a number of other requirements of the comet watcher: Binoculars can offer extraordinarily bright images with relatively large fields of view.

"Field of view" is a term that comes up often in the world of comet watching. It refers to the expanse of sky an instrument will take in. Typically in

comet watching, what you're looking for is a broad
field of view: The comet is not like a planet, a tiny
spot in the sky that can only be seen well with good
magnification. It is a broad object with a tail stretching across the heavens. You want to see big pieces of
this object and see them clearly. Wide field of view
also makes it much easier to aim at an object in the
sky and capture it because the image delivered to the
eye is so large. And it is useful, even mandatory, to
have a wide field of view when the object is moving
across the field or you are. (That is to say, if you are
trying to steady the instrument with your hands un-
assisted by a tripod, you will be moving despite your
best efforts, and the images in the sky will tend to
race in and out of your field of vision unless you can
see a lot of the sky at once.)

Field of view is measured in degrees that can be
imagined with some accuracy if you keep in mind
that the full moon is about ½ degree. So binoculars
with a 7-degree field of view would be seeing a
chunk of the sky 14 full moons wide. By comparison, a standard home telescope might give you
something in the vicinity of 1 degree. Generally
speaking, the higher the magnification, the narrower
the field of view. So for watching Halley's it makes
sense to purchase binoculars that are not ballyhooed
for their power.

The power of binoculars is given to you as the first
of two figures. A 10 x 25 pair has a power of 10. That
means it magnifies the image 10 times what the human eye would ordinarily see. The second figure is
the diameter in millimeters of the objective lens—
the lens at the front of the binoculars that gathers
light. Binoculars are sometimes sold with incredibly
high power, of 30 or 35.

But the binoculars that astronomers often recommend for comet watching are in the 7 x 50 range (8 x
56 is fine, too). Binoculars with these specifications
offer adequate, but relatively low magnification.

They have in general a field of view from 7 to 10 degrees.

At least as important as the ability to capture a large area of the sky is the ability of some binoculars to deliver an extraordinarily bright image, capitalizing on a fascinating aspect of astronomical observation. Astronomers often talk about something called an exit pupil. That is the size of the beam of light leaving the eyepiece of the binoculars. The larger the exit pupil, all other things being equal, the brighter the image. Large exit pupils are especially useful in conditions offering low light. But the human eye can make use of only so much light. In daylight, before the visual purple has bathed the retina to make it light sensitive and when the pupil of the eye is closed down in response to sunlight, the retina is receptive to an exit pupil of only 2 millimeters. At night, when the eye has been fully dark-adapted, it can accept an exit pupil as large as 7 millimeters. That's the most efficient beam of light, too, because a larger exit pupil would be wasted on the eye. One way to test binoculars' suitability for nighttime use is to view an image at dusk with the naked eye and then with the binoculars and see whether the image has actually gained substantially in brightness—as it should—with the use of the glasses.

Binoculars, depending in part on whether they're meant to be used mostly in daylight or for astronomy, offer exit pupils of differing magnitude. The way to determine the exit pupil of a specific piece of equipment is to divide the power (the first number) into the objective lens diameter (the second number). Thus it can be seen that binoculars designated 7 x 50 deliver an exit pupil that is very close to the maximum the eye might accept. (During World War II, binoculars of these dimensions were called night glasses; a pair of 7 x 35 binoculars, meant for daytime use, will not give you a very bright image at all.) Higher magnification would require a larger ob-

jective lens to do the same thing. There are in fact
larger binoculars on the market—some of them are
called giant binoculars in the manufacturers' bro-
chures—that offer roughly the desired exit pupil, between 7 and 8, with more magnification, a power of
10 or 11. But that power requires an objective lens of
80 millimeters. The field of view is forced to shrink
from 7 or so (in 7 x 50 binoculars) to 4.5, and the
weight of the instrument goes up considerably, to
perhaps 5 pounds from the 2 to 4 pounds typical in
standard-size binoculars. There are those observers
who definitely prefer the added magnification and
will accept some awkwardness and a diminished
field of view to get it. Needless to say, the big binoculars are useless handheld and require a tripod.

Actually, a tripod is a good idea regardless, and the
market offers tripods especially made for binoculars.
These have small legs and need to be propped up on
something like a railing. An ordinary camera tripod,
with proper adapter, will work well. Muirden prefers
to haul a comfortable reclining armchair out into
the backyard and stabilize himself and his binoculars in luxury. That makes spectacular sense as long
as your backyard is dark enough, of course.

When it comes to choosing a specific pair of binoculars, we have a few notions on how to go about it.

As for brand names, there is one astronomer we
know who swears by his Leitz and another raves
about his Nikon. Suffice it to say, without intending
anything like a specific endorsement, that the top of
the line made by the likes of Nikon, Leitz, and
Bausch & Lomb (and its allied brand, Bushnell) are
widely admired. If you can't or don't wish to spend
the money required for one of these beauties, at least
familiarize yourself with them so that as you dip
down into the more modest price ranges, you have
some feeling for the way the better pieces of equipment perform.

But don't bother with anything that is downright

cheap. Good binoculars can't be truly cheap. They require too many precision parts. If the components are not properly aligned, they deliver double images. Or cheap binoculars might have inferior prisms that produce a phenomenon known as astigmatism, in which a focused star looks like a tiny cross. A bad eyepiece is as good as none at all, blurring the image.

As you shop, it is possible to check for poor alignment of the components. Focus on an object several hundred feet away and then carefully move the binoculars away from you while still staring through the instrument. The farther away you can hold the binoculars from your eyes while still seeing a single image, the better is the alignment. A distance of an arm's length should be enough to provide an adequate assessment.

Test the binoculars for comfort. You should be happy with the adjustments at the eyepieces and in the center, and you should like the way the binoculars rest against your eyes. Some of them are far easier to use with eyeglasses than are others, and this can be an important consideration.

## *What About Telescopes?*

For one thing, telescopes represent a greater commitment to sky watching than do binoculars. They are more expensive, less portable, and more specific for the job at hand, observing the heavens. Many astronomical telescopes (as opposed to the terrestrial variety) deliver an inverted view; that's rarely much of a problem in observing celestial objects, but it is unacceptable if you give up on the sky and try to turn it to more mundane observations here on Earth.

Telescopes also offer a smaller field of view than do binoculars, and yet that should not rule them out altogether. In conjunction with a good pair of binoculars, for instance, a telescope, with its greater magnification, might allow you to zoom in on some particularly interesting facet of the comet, one of those kinks in the cometary tail, for instance. And, in any case, some telescopes are much better suited for comet watching than others.

In setting out to purchase a telescope, one is immediately confronted by the terminology used for its anatomy. So here's a quick rundown on what that's all about.

All telescopes, like all binoculars, do essentially the same thing: They gather light much more efficiently than the naked eye, and that is their major function. They direct that light through a magnifying element in the eyepiece. Magnification is not nearly so important as good light gathering (usually magnification is a simple matter of finding the eyepiece to deliver the size image you need; astronomers recommend that you never use a magnifying power that is greater than 40 times the diameter of the objective lens). The light gathering is done in two major ways: through refraction or through reflection. Refraction refers to light collected through a lens. Reflection refers to light collected by a mirror.

Generally speaking, when teachers of astronomy are asked which kind of telescope makes most sense for the beginner, they point unhesitatingly toward *reflectors*, or a modified reflector called a catadiop-

## KEPLERIAN REFRACTOR

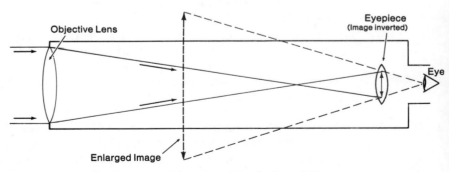

In a refractor telescope, the light passes directly through the lenses.

**CLASSICAL CASSEGRAIN**

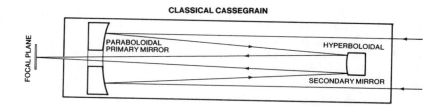

**NEWTONIAN REFLECTOR**

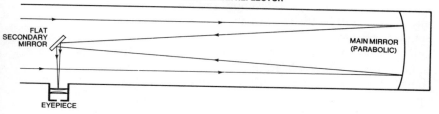

tric telescope. The reasons for preferring reflectors are several. Lenses are a great deal more expensive to make well than are mirrors. One obvious reason is that they have two surfaces (both sides of the lens) that need to be ground to perfection. Moreover, the light will be passing through the lens rather than simply bouncing off it, and that means the lens glass must be of extraordinarily high quality. In addition, most good quality refractor telescopes require additional lenses to correct for distorted color reception known as chromatic aberration (still more work for the manufacturer). Thus reflecting telescopes are much simpler devices, and you get more efficiency for the money.

The main difficulty that inventors of the reflector had to overcome was to devise a way to get an image on the front of the mirror to the eye (which, for obvious reasons could not be in front of the mirror), and they achieved that with the development of a secondary mirror. One approach, called the Cassegrain after the French physician Giovanni Cassegrain, uses a secondary mirror positioned in front of the main mirror, and it reflects the gathered light through a small hole in the main mirror and then to the eye. The Cassegrain design is very compact.

The second major type of reflector is the Newtonian, after Isaac Newton, who built it first. In the Newtonian arrangement, the secondary mirror picks up the beam of light and directs it to a point outside the tube, usually directly to the side. The effect is strange for first-time users who expect to place their eye to the rear of the telescope and peer straight ahead as would be the case in a refractor or in a Cassegrain reflector.

Reflectors usually have an open front end that makes them vulnerable in an accident and exposes their mirrors to dust and other insults. The catadioptric, or compound telescope, as it is sometimes called, is a reflector telescope, usually of the Cassegrain type, that also employs a front lens. The secondary mirror is attached to the front lens. Thus the catadioptric, which is closed to dust and larger objects, is especially sturdy.

The kind of telescope that is best suited to comet watching is known generically as a rich field telescope, often referred to as an RFT. These are short instruments of relatively low power with an extraordinary (for a telescope) field of view. A rich field telescope can be expected to have a field of view in the vicinity of 2.5 to 3 degrees, an area covering six full moons, although this is still less than half the field of view offered by many binoculars. While not providing an especially large image, they can bring wonderful brightness to a sky that offers only muted contrast when viewed by the naked eye.

The demand for these telescopes as Comet Halley approaches is bound to be great. When Celestron came out with its Comet Catcher ($469)—an RFT weighing a mere 6.4 pounds and only 20 inches long—the popularity was instant. Stephen Edberg of the Jet Propulsion Laboratory reviewed it in *Astron-*

*omy,* and he found this instrument to be one he could recommend heartily, although he felt it had several shortcomings. Among them: It wasn't as easy to hold as it should have been, and the tripod mount was poorly placed, making the telescope more awkward to use than need be. In any event, this is far from the only RFT on the market (Edmund Scientific, for instance, has a catalog that describes a number of such telescopes), and it makes sense to compare it with others that are perhaps less cleverly named.

For those who already have a telescope or who wish to get a telescope with more conventional stargazing properties, the simple purchase of a wide-angle or rich field adapter will certainly help. It can double the field of view of your telescope while halving its magnification.

An interesting accessory that is widely available is a light-pollution filter, which manages to reject the radiation from mercury and high- and low-pressure sodium lights.

Once you've invested in an optical instrument specifically with Halley's Comet in mind, you may wonder what good it will be later on. Perhaps surprisingly, both binoculars and rich field telescopes have a great many astronomical uses. They make for enjoyable observation of the Moon, for instance, providing a wider image than most telescopes would. Beyond the Moon, they are excellent for observing deep-space objects, like the Orion Nebula and the Pleiades star cluster. They are fine for looking at the Milky Way, at the moons of Jupiter, the phases of Venus or the Andromeda Galaxy. In other words, they provide a superb way to roam the heavens. (And, of course, binoculars are ideal for bird-watching and, perhaps, for watching horse races.)

And then there are always the comets. Comet watching has itself become a specialty among amateurs of every stripe. The Comet Digest feature in

the magazine *Sky & Telescope,* for instance, is a re-
pository of ongoing data collecting. In a report in
that magazine on Comet Kopff's apparition in 1983,
John Bortle told of his experience in first spotting
the comet on its return toward Earth, and of the data
he received from observers around the world. He
said he received 250 magnitude estimates (accomplished amateurs as well as professionals learn to
judge the brightness magnitude of a celestial body by
comparing it with the known magnitudes of other
objects) and from them he was able to determine
that "Comet Kopff is intrinsically much brighter
and more active than most of the other short-period
comets."

So for those who find that Comet Halley whets
their appetite, the wait for something else to do with
all that newfound excitement and learning and
equipment need not be anything like seventy-six
years.

# Coverage of
# The New York Times

## 1910, Day by Day

In 1910 Comet Halley brought with it a measure of enjoyment and wonder, shrouded in confusion, fear, and pessimism. And when it was gone, one journalistic account says that the only tangible thing it left behind "along Broadway" was the Comet Club formed at the Knickerbocker Hotel. Well, neither the club nor the hotel is here anymore either. But these journalistic accounts—funny, cryptic, and informative—remain in full.

### August 25, 1909

#### EXPECTING HALLEY'S COMET

##### Lick Observatory Watching for Return
##### of the Periodic Visitor

LICK OBSERVATORY, MOUNT HAMILTON, Cal., Aug. 24 — Keen rivalry has developed among the astronomers of the world and all through the night every available telescope is sweeping the heavens to gain the first sight of the returning Halley's Comet. Owing to the high power "comet seeking" glasses on Mount Hamilton, the Lick astronomers expect to announce the return of Halley's Comet after its 75 years' absence from the solar system.

In the years between 1895 and 1905, of the 38 comets discovered by the astronomers of the world, twelve were first sighted by Lick observers.

## September 13, 1909
## PAGE 1

### HALLEY'S COMET SEEN

#### *Heidelberg Observer the First to Catch Sight of It*

CAMBRIDGE, Mass., Sept. 12 — Halley's Comet, for which astronomers the world over have been eagerly watching, has been seen, after an absence of seventy years, according to a dispatch received today at the Harvard Observatory from Prof. Wolff of Heidelberg. The sight was obtained Sept. 11, in a right ascension six hours, 18 minutes, 12 seconds; declination 17 degrees 11 minutes north. It could be made out only with a large telescope.

Halley's Comet has been one of the important phenomena in the history of astronomy. Chinese and European astronomers noticed comet appearances in 1378, 1456, 1531, and 1607, but no one thought of associating them until Edmund Halley, the son of a London soap maker, identified them in 1682. Halley founded the science of cometic identification. By means of his system, recurring comets are now identified by determining their inclination, the longitude of their nodes, the longitude of their perihelions, their perihelion distances, and the direction of their motion.

If it is really Halley's Comet which Prof. Wolff has sighted, it seems to be reappearing somewhat early. It is supposed to reappear every seventy-six years.

## December 25, 1909
## PAGE 1

### HALLEY'S COMET MISSHAPEN

#### *Prof. Lowell's Photograph Shows the*
#### *Nucleus Is Out the Centre*

BOSTON, Dec. 24 — Dispatches from Flagstaff, Ariz., state that Prof. Percival Lowell has successfully photographed Halley's Comet. The picture shows an irregular formation, but with a distinct nucleus, which is out of the centre.

## January 25, 1910
## PAGE 1

### NEW COMET RECEDING

*Five Photographs Taken at Harvard*
*Last Night Show the Movement*

BOSTON, Jan. 24 — The bright rival of Venus in the western sky, the new comet first seen from Johannesburg, and known officially as Comet A. 1910, is receding according to photographs taken by the Harvard Observatory to-night.

## January 25, 1910
## EDITORIAL

### CONFUSING THE COMETS

The comet some clear-sighted folks say they have seen near the western horizon of late is not HALLEY'S Comet, but an unidentified butter-in from space, now called for convenience "A. 1910," which is as good a name as any for a comet without a history. Somewhere in the neighborhood is Daniel's comet "A. 1909," another hitherto uncatalogued traveler in space. Both may be older than HALLEY'S comet, but neither is closely identified with the delusions of man, or his slow development in science.

For centuries the comet now named for the great astronomer of Newton's era pursued a successful though fraudulent career as a portent of evil and a warning to wicked men. It flamed over Rome when Caesar had been killed in the Capitol and incited the populace, more surely than any crafty speech of Marc Anthony "to cry havoc and let slip the dogs of war." Since the Norman conquest of England, its comings and goings have been pretty accurately determined, and HALLEY seems to have been one of the first of the astronomers to study it scientifically. It is now a well-known comet, and has given up the portent game, minding its own business and keeping its stellar engagements as well as could be expected.

The only comet in the heavens now visible to the naked eye is the intruder called "A. 1910." It may have been "A. 1910 B.C.," for all we know, but it is new to us, and as a stranger we give it welcome. But we are justified in regarding it with some suspicion. It comes unheralded, and it demands a great deal of careful investigation. We may well doubt its possession of evil powers, but we must not confuse it with a steady-going old comet like HALLEY's, which has long outlived the misdeeds of its youth, for which it was not entirely responsible, and comes into view every seventy-five years or so with the same cheerful aspect. Until a new Federal bureau is established at Washington to see that all comets are properly branded with the owner's name, we must be cautious.

## January 29, 1910

### NEW COMET HAS TWO TAILS

#### So. Arizona University Observer
#### Reports of "A. 1910"

TUCSON, Ariz., Jan. 28 — Prof. A. E. Douglas, observer at the University of Arizona, reports that comet "A. 1910" is doubletailed. Wednesday night the second tail was noted branching off due south, with the other pointing straight upward. Prof. Douglas estimated the length of the double tail at 28 degrees, the longest since the comet of 1882.

GUADALAJARA, Mexico, Jan 28 — With the appearance of "Comet A. 1910" pilgrimages to the shrine of the Virgin of Talpa are being organized, many of the pilgrims making the journey for miles on their knees. Talpa is in the western section of the State of Jalisco, and pilgrimages are made annually to the shrine.

Advices from several points state that consternation reigns among the more superstitious class.

## EDITORIAL

### BOYCOTT THE SALT COMET

The comet labeled A. 1910, which is not included in the authentic catalogue of 22 identified comets, 14 with periods ranging from 4 to 14 years, and 8 with periods of from 32 to 76 years, is causing a great deal of perplexity, as might have been expected. Few have seen it, but all know it is there, as Mr. George Sampson remarked of Miss Lavina Wilfer's flannel petticoat. Those who have seen it pronounce strange things concerning it. One spectroscopic artist has discovered sodium, an element hitherto lacking in well-ordered comets, in A. 1910. It is just possible that some alert scientist has been putting salt on its tail, but it is more likely that this strangely perverse comet has a lot of things in its composition which do not belong to other comets. A salt comet is certainly a novelty. No wonder the simple, credulous Mexicans are scared. It has two tails, one of them of extraordinary length. Its behavior from the beginning has been unlike that of the catalogued comets.

We do not believe for a moment that its appearance should cause any appre-hension, because comets are all arrant humbugs, the tails of which do not blaze at all, but only seem to, while their heads are as light as any known to the best society, and their bodies non-existent. But it would serve this comet right if it were wholly ignored. That would teach it a lesson. This year of 1910 belongs exclusively, according to the astronomers, to the big comet called Halley's. The program of performances this Summer by Halley's Comet was arranged more than seventy years ago and appeared in the textbooks when one's grandfather went to school. It will be carried out with no postponement on account of indisposition or the weather.

But some months before the scheduled time for Halley's Comet to reveal itself to the unaided eye this double-tailed, well-salted hobo of the heavens wanders into our ken and rashly assumes responsibility for the floods and fires and strikes and the high cost of living, without any historical authority what-ever. The wine of 1910 will be remarkably good, because comet-year wine is always better than that of other years, and Halley's Comet was prepared to take the credit for it. We know what Halley's Comet has already done for the world, since it outgrew its old evil ways. Let us stick to Halley's and boycott the unheralded comet.

## February 8, 1910
## PAGE 1

### COMET'S POISONOUS TAIL

#### Yerkes Observatory Finds Cyanogen In
#### Spectrum of Halley's Comet

SPECIAL TO THE NEW YORK TIMES

BOSTON, Mass., Feb. 7 — Astronomers at the Harvard Observatory have not yet made a photographic spectrum of Halley's Comet, which is rapidly ap-proaching the Earth, but a telegram received there to-day from the Yerkes Observatory states that spectra of the comet obtained by the Director and his assistants show very prominent cyanogen bands.

Cyanogen is a very deadly poison, a grain of its potassium salt touched to the tongue being sufficient to cause instant death. In the uncombined state it is a bluish gas very similar in its chemical behavior to chlorine and extremely poisonous. It is characterized by an odor similar to that of almonds. The fact that cyanogen is present in the comet has been communicated to Camille Flammarion and many other astronomers, and is causing much discussion as to the probable effect on the Earth should it pass through the comet's tail. Prof. Flammarion is of the opinion that the cyanogen gas would impregnate the atmosphere and possibly snuff out all life on the planet.

Only once as far as known, has the Earth passed directly through the tail of a comet, and at that time no unusual phenomena were noticed except that there were abundant showers of meteors. Most astronomers do not agree with Flammarion, inasmuch as the tail of a comet is in a state of almost inconceivable rarification, and believe that it would be repelled by the mass of the Earth as it is by the light of the Sun. Also it is considered probable that the cyanogen of the comet's tail on contact with the Earth's atmosphere would be decomposed by combustion into nitrogen and carbon dioxide, in quantities quite harmless to animal life.

## February 11, 1910
## EDITORIAL

### TOPICS OF THE TIMES
#### *Poison in the Tail of a Comet*

People who were disturbed by the recent news that the "cyanogen line" had been found in the spectrum in the tail of Halley's Comet by the astronomers at the Yerkes Observatory have now been kindly relieved of their anxiety by Prof. Hussey of the University of Michigan. He does not deny that cyanogen is a most terrible poison or that a comet would not have to add much of it to our atmosphere to destroy very promptly all terrestrial life. He only calls attention to the fact—which anybody, by the way, can find in any recent astronomical work—that the tails of comets are of such almost inconceivable tenuity, and that even though they were composed of nothing but cyanogen the Earth could pass through a dozen of them without producing the slightest effect upon the most delicate of its inhabitants.

Cometary tails are so near to nothing at all that the thinnest mist of which we have any knowledge is grossly material in comparison. The spectroscope's verdict is always beyond question, and wherever it finds cyanogen or anything else there the thing indicated by the "lines" undoubtedly exists, but the discovery, though sure, may mean amazingly little as to quantity, and such is undoubtedly the case in regard to comets. Only to ignorance or superstition are they alarming.

## April 9, 1910
## PAGE 1

### HALLEY'S COMET REAPPEARS

#### *Emerging from Glows of Sun's Disk*
#### *Not Yet Visible to the Naked Eye*

SAN JOSE, Cal., April 8 — Halley's comet was observed through the Lick Telescope on Mount Hamilton about daylight to-day, but only the head could be seen, as the tail was lost in the bright background of the rising Sun. The comet will not be visible to the naked eye for several days.

CAPETOWN, April 8 — The observatory here sighted Halley's Comet this morning for the first time since its passing the Sun.

Prof. Harold Jacoby, Rutherfurd Professor of Astronomy at Columbia, speaking last night of the reappearance of Halley's Comet after passing the Sun, said it was impossible to predict definitely when it would be visible to the naked eye. All depended, he said, on the rate with which its brightness increased as it approached the Sun. He thought it would probably be at least two weeks before it could be seen here without a telescope.

## April 30, 1910

### PROGRESS OF THE COMET

#### Visitor Sighted at Sea—Also Aids
#### Jersey Chicken Thieves

BY UNITED WIRELESS TO THE NEW YORK TIMES

S.S. ARAPAHOE, off Cape Hatteras, April 29 — The first officer of the *Arapahoe*, Mr. Darling, saw Halley's Comet this morning at 3:30 o'clock, the ship being then ten miles above Cape Lookout, bound north. The comet was hardly discernable with the naked eye, but was easily made out with glasses. The tail inclined toward the southeast, and was circular toward the end. It was seen due east, 15 degrees up from the horizon.

Scientists prophesied that the proximity of Halley's Comet would be detrimental to the wireless service, but the operators of both the land and ship stations report that this week they have been doing the best long distance work for several weeks.

SPECIAL TO THE NEW YORK TIMES

NEW BRUNSWICK, N. J., April 29 — Prof. R. W. Prentiss, Astronomer at Rutgers College, saw Halley's Comet this morning between 2:30 and 4 o'clock from his home in Highland Park. He could make out the comet with his naked eye, he reported, though it was not conspicuously bright. A heavy mist obscured the comet somewhat. Prof. Prentiss said that the comet's tail was about two degrees long, and the comet seemed to be about four times as big as an ordinary star. It was due east, slightly to the left and above Venus.

SPECIAL TO THE NEW YORK TIMES

TOWACO, N.J., April 29 — Two well dressed young men passed through here yesterday, telling everybody they met that this morning, between midnight and sunrise, Halley's Comet, with a long tail, would be visible from the top of Waukhaw Mountain, and that the scientific school which they represented would give prizes for the best amateur descriptions of the comet and its tail.

There was not much interest in these prizes until the word ran around that Lily Lautergan, Cyrus Lautergan's more than talented daughter, was going to the top of the mountain, with her easel and palette, and there make a sketch of the comet, its tail and all its environment and background.

Mary Vanderlip, daughter of Josh Vanderlip, said that the teacher at school had declared that, as far as sky coloring was concerned, she was equal to and most likely superior to Lily Lautergan.

Well, anyway, this morning Waukhaw Mountain top was covered with Towaco's beauty and chivalry and chaperonage. Miss Lily and Miss Mary were ready with their palettes, with bets on the winner. A good time was not had on Waukhaw Mountain top. Halley's Comet was not seen, and when Towaco's citizenry got back down to their homes they found that their chicken coops had been looted. Cyrus Doolite lost 300 fowls, and both the Lautergan and Vanderlip families were heavy losers.

"Halley's Comets can go to the dickens, as far as I'm concerned," said Mr. Lautergan, after he counted his losses. "Doggone comets anyhow."

"Don't be rude, father," said Lily. "It hurts me. Those young gentlemen were not chicken thieves."

**Paris Reports on Comet**

PARIS, April 29 — The Astronomical Society announces that Halley's Comet is now visible in Paris between 3:15 and 3:50 A.M. Its form is that of a clouded star.

## May 5, 1910

### SAYS EARTH IS IN NO DANGER

#### No Fear of Collision with the Comet—
#### Prof. Jacoby Proves It

Schermerhorn Hall at Columbia University was not big enough to accommodate all those who desired to hear Prof. Harold Jacoby tell the wonders of Halley's Comet yesterday afternoon. He demonstrated by a model of Sir William Herschel's that the inhabitants of this Earth need have no fear of a collision. While it is true, said Prof. Jacoby, that the comet is rapidly moving nearer, the Earth is in no danger.

On May 19, Prof. Jacoby declares, the comet will be midway between the Earth and the Sun, so that a straight line would cut the three bodies. . . .

Several experiments greatly interested the audience, especially one in which Prof. Jacoby, with a magnetic coil under a glass surface, illustrated the way a comet is attracted by the forces of gravity.

When shot from a tiny toy cannon with no magnetic force to influence it, the small ball simply rolled in a straight line. But when the current was turned on, the ball took the oval, cometary motion.

## May 9, 1910

### COMET SCARE IN BERMUDA

#### *Celestial Visitor Seen Acting Strangely Soon After King Edward's Death*

Queer things seemed to be going on around Halley's Comet about the time of the accession of King George V., according to observations in Bermuda, news of which was received here last night by United Wireless from the steamship Bermudian, now at sea.

According to the dispatch on Friday night, the night of the death of King Edward and the accession of his son, the comet became visible in Bermuda at 2 o'clock in the morning, and a decidedly red tinge was noted in its tail. At 12:30 that night the fort at Hamilton, Bermuda, began to fire a salute of 101 guns in honor of the new King. An interval of two minutes elapsed between each discharge and so the final gun was fired at 3:52 exactly.

As the report died away, the observer saw a sudden flaring up at the end of the comet's tail. The head also glowed, a ball of red fire. For five minutes the phenomenon lasted, and was seen by the negroes at work on the docks. They were overcome with terror. They fell on their knees and began to pray. They thought that the end of the world was surely coming, and it was impossible to get them to go on with the loading of the Bermudian.

Some of them connected the strange light with the death of King Edward. It showed, they declared, that war was sure to break out in King George's reign, and that some great calamity would befall the Earth. They were speechless with fear and worked themselves up in their paroxysms of religious zeal to a perfect frenzy. It was not till the comet had faded from view and the daylight of Saturday had broken that they could be induced to go on again with their work.

## May 14, 1910

### USE HOTEL ROOFS
### FOR COMET PARTIES

*Clerks Kept Busy Calling Guests*
*Who Wished to Get a View*
*of the Visitor*

### NOVEL FEAST AT GOTHAM

*Amateur Astronomers Had Breakfast*
*In an Improvised Bower While*
*an Orchestra Played*

The interest in Halley's Comet, the tail of which will engulf the Earth in four days, has finally reached the guests of the hotels, and the roofs of all the big ones are crowded nightly now by comet parties. A guest at the Hotel Gotham gave a breakfast early yesterday morning to his friends on the roof of the hotel, and the occasion was enlivened with music. . . .

A woman who registered at the Plaza asked for a room on the top floor, where she could watch the comet. . . .

There was a jolly comet party on the roof of the Hotel Astor. . . . The women all wore their furs, while the men were bundled up so as to resemble inhabitants of the polar regions.

### MITCHELL RIDICULES
### FEAR OF THE COMET

*Columbia Astronomer Tells Thirteen*
*Club It Has Aroused*
*the Superstitious for Ages*

### THINKS HOMER KNEW OF IT

*Coincidences in the History of the Visitor*
*Pointed Out—Two Last Visits*
*Spanned Mark Twain's Life*

With Prof. S. A. Mitchell, adjunct Professor of Astrology at Columbia University, aiding and abetting, the Thirteen Club, dedicated to knocking on the head all superstitions connected with May, Friday, and thirteen, spent most of last night trying to pluck the sting from Halley's Comet, which, Prof. Mitchell said, was known to have been frightening people since B.C. 240.

The Thirteen Club held its dinner and seance afterward in the "Garret" restaurant, on the twenty-third floor of the West Street Building, 90 West Street. The club has 813 members. Last night 169 were present, and they sat at thirteen tables, thirteen at each one. And, as Prof. Mitchell observed, it was Friday, May the "unlucky" month, and the 13th. Not only so, but each member spilled salt on the table, and as many as possible sat under big umbrellas raised at the head of each table.

Prof. Mitchell made a distinct contribution to gone superstitions early in the address on the comet, which, according to tradition, has always been preceded or accompanied on its visits by war, bloodshed, pestilence, and calamity, saying the comet would rise this morning at 2:47 o'clock, and these figures being added make thirteen. . . .

Homer knew of this comet, Prof. Mitchell said, and he quoted the lines in the Iliad familiar to classical scholars, referring to it:

> Like the red star, that from his flaming
> hair
> Shakes down disease, pestilence, and war . . .
> Iliad, xix., 381.

[Prof. Mitchell] took a shot at the old-time doctors, saying he had just been reading an interesting book in which a learned physician said he always prescribed rhubarb for his patients when a comet was expected or visible. . . .

"There is no doubt in the world," he said, "that the comet's tail contains cyanogen gas, found in prussic acid, a poison so powerful that a drop on the tongue would cause instant death. The spectrum shows it plainly. Very probably some of you would like to take to a dugout or subcellar that day. If you are really so afraid that you are all going to die on that day, I hope you will make your bank accounts over to me, as I am willing to take my chances."

Then, after bringing his audience up to a high tension he told them that a comet was as nearly an airy nothing as one could well imagine. . . . This being the case there was not the slightest danger, he said, from the cyanogen gas in the tail, for this gas would be mixed with the Earth's atmosphere, thereby still further attenuating it. He also relieved the tension of his audience's feelings to some extent by recalling that the Earth had already passed through two tails of comets, namely in 1819 and in 1861, and the people did not even know about it.

## VENUS MISTAKEN FOR THE COMET

TO THE EDITOR OF THE NEW YORK TIMES

Your paper has kept its readers well informed of the movements of Halley's Comet. I think this is the first report you have received of its having been sighted in the heart of the Catskills. A party of us at the Silver Stream Cottage arose at 3 o'clock Sunday morning to see the newcomer. At just 8:22 the fiery ball was seen to make its appearance above the horizon, over the ridge of hills just east of Tonshi Mountain, beneath and just a little to the right of Aquarius.

There was no tail in sight, not even by the aid of powerful field glasses, but at times there seemed to be flashes of brilliancy more intense. We observed the wanderer until 4:15 and during this time it did not seem to change its aspect.

FREDERICK J. REHN

WEST SHOKAN, N.Y., May 12, 1910

The brilliant, tailless object our friend saw beneath Aquarius was Venus, not the comet—EDITOR TIMES.

## COMET VIEW FROM BALLOON

### R. C. Tripp Starts Off with Friends for a Sight from Cloudland

Roswell C. Tripp, ex-Yale athlete and member of several successive All-American football teams, now a downtown broker, left the Grand Central station last night with a few college friends for Springfield, Mass., where he had previously chartered the balloon Springfield for a comet-seeing exhibition. Pilot Arnold, winner of the International race held in Vienna last year, has been retained to manage the ascent. . . .

One of the members of the party said last night:

"Mr. Tripp is the only one of us who has ever seen a balloon, but we have been training in the Harvard Club gymnasium for the last week, and we think we can make the proper leap from the basket at the proper time. We will be equipped with photographic and telescopic instruments, and intend to make this a scientific as well as a novel adventure.

"It is our intention to stay up in the air as long as practicable."

## INVOLUNTARY STAR GAZERS

### Mount Holly's New Fire Whistle Got Folks Out to See the Comet

MOUNT HOLLY, N.J., May 13 — All in Mount Holly saw the comet this morning, although they had no intention of gazing at it when they retired last night. The brand-new fire whistle, which was installed yesterday, awoke them at 3:25 this morning. Everybody jumped out of bed to see the fire. The blaze was in the Mount Holly Boat Clubhouse, on Water Street, but the firemen could do little to save it.

After the fire had died down the early risers wended their way back toward home, when some one mentioned the comet, and then all looked for and saw it, so they say, and then they continued to their homes and to bed again.

## MAY 15, 1910
## LEAD STORY, PAGE 1

### WATCHING THE COMET
### ALL OVER THE WORLD

*And Speculating on the Probability of the Earth's*
*Passing Through Its Tail*

### THERE'S DOUBT ABOUT IT

*Oxford Professor Says the Tail Is Too*
*Short to Reach Us—American*
*Estimates Make It Long*
*Enough and to Spare*

SPECIAL CABLE TO THE NEW YORK TIMES

LONDON, May 14 — Halley's Comet to-day is about 26,000,000 miles from the Earth, toward which it is rushing at a rate which will bring it to the nearest point to the Earth on Wednesday next. On that day, if the tail be 15,000,000 miles in length, the Earth will pass through the tail. The latest observations here lead astronomers to conclude that the Earth may not come into contact with the comet's tail, which is calculated by British astronomers to be only 7,500,000 miles long. The measurement of a comet's tail, however, depends upon the fortunate situation of the observer, and if American estimates of 20,000,000 to 25,000,000 miles are correct, the Earth, of course, will pass through the tail on May 18.

The diameter of the comet's head is estimated to be about 9,000 miles—not much greater than that of the Earth.

That the tail may come up to the previous expectations as to its length before May 18 is indicated by recent observations by means of the spectroscope. These show a strange transformation, which must be added to the number of cometary mysteries which await explanation. For several weeks the spectrum of the comet showed the presence of hydrocarbons and cyanogen only, but now the existence of a large quantity of sodium is revealed.

Signs that will show whether the filmy tail does envelope the world on the night of May 18 will not be such as to cause any alarm. Herbert Hall Turner, Savilian Professor of Astronomy at Oxford University, says it is impossible to state with any certainty whether any influence may be detected on May 18.

"Possibly," he says, "delicate instruments for recording atmospheric electricity might show some disturbance; possibly, if there are solid particles in the tail, a few meteors might be seen. Possibly nothing will happen at all, and that last alternative is by far the most likely for, according to recent observations, the tail is far too short to reach us."

## FRENCH ARE MUCH DISTURBED

BY MARCONI TRANSATLANTIC WIRELESS TELEGRAPH TO THE NEW YORK TIMES

PARIS, May 14 — The weather and Halley's Comet have recently occupied a very large space in the imagination of Parisians. It is not that it has required any great imaginative effort to appreciate the enormities which the weather has been committing, but the minds of the people persistently dwell upon the theoretical connection between the weather and the comet, and from this occupation the attitude of the majority of scientists who have spoken or written on the subject has not diverted them.

Science has to admit, although rather negatively than positively, that the approach of the comet is very likely, in large degree, to be the cause of the remarkable meteorological perturbations to which Western Europe, more particularly France, has been subject in the last few weeks.

What further will the comet do to the inhabitants of the Earth? . . .

## TRIPP'S LONG FLIGHT TO-DAY

### *Obtains 60,000 Cubic Feet of Long-Distance Balloon Gas from Pittsfield*

PITTSFIELD, Mass., May 14 — Not being able to secure long-distance balloon gas in Springfield, Mass., Roswell C. Tripp, the big Yale football guard of a few years ago, with his guests, Fairman Dick of New York and Edward C. Ely of Norwich, Conn., changed the base of the balloon trip from Springfield to this city to-day, and will start on a 200-mile flight at 2 o'clock to-morrow morning. . . .

## MAY 15, 1910
## LETTER TO THE EDITOR

### "BURNING DAYLIGHT"

### *The Household is Greatly Stirred Up*
### *Over the Mystery*

TO THE EDITOR OF THE NEW YORK TIMES:

The comet can't be avoided, but surely something can be done about this "Burning Daylight" plague that has descended on the city.

I have been deeply stirred during the week by the receipt of the red ink warnings. "Only so many days to Burning Daylight" and [I] have appealed in vain to the police. Now I come to you.

It's this way: Our servant girl is scared helpless about the comet, my wife is sure "Burning Daylight" is something terrible, my daughter, being romantic, laughs at both the comet and the red ink, while I, the only man about the house, have to combat a combination of tears, shudders and indifference.

Personally, I am not satisfied that "Burning Daylight" means anything serious, but my wife is of a different opinion and wants me to cast about for light on the mystery. Can I get some?

PERPLEXED

New York, May 12, 1910

## MAY 16, 1910
## LEAD STORY PAGE 1

### IN COMET'S TAIL
### ON WEDNESDAY

*European And American Astronomers
Agree the Earth Will
Not Suffer in the Passage*

### TELL THE TIMES ABOUT IT

*And of Proposed Observations—Yerkes
Observatory to Use Balloons if the Weather's Cloudy*

### TAIL 46,000,000 MILES LONG?

*Scarfed in a Filmy Bit of It, We'll
Whirl On in Our Dance Through
Space, Unharmed, and, Most
of Us, Unheeding*

*The views of European and American astronomers, sent to The New York Times by cable and telegraph, on the probable effect upon the Earth of its passage through the tail of Halley's Comet, appear below. That there will be no effect upon animal or vegetable life, perhaps no perceptible effect of any kind, is generally agreed; but there may be meteoric and electrical manifestations. It is pointed out that the comet's tail is so tenuous that it probably does not contain more than a single solid particle or gaseous molecule to the cubic yard. . . .*

*Recent estimates have put the length of the tail at 20,000,000 to 40,000,000 miles. To reach the Earth, it must exceed 15,000,000 miles. The Earth is due to enter the tail on Wednesday night at 11:20 o'clock, and to emerge from it two hours later.*

SPECIAL CABLE TO THE NEW YORK TIMES
LONDON, May 15 — Halley's Comet, which has seemed the harbinger of so many misfortunes since 2616 B.C., the traditional year of Methusaleh's death, when, according to Sir Robert Hall, it visited terrestrial regions, reaches its climax of interest for this generation this week, in the course of which it crosses the Sun's disk, makes its nearest approach to the Earth, and rises first in the night sky.

It is now calculated that its nearest approach to the Earth will be on Saturday, when it will be only 14,300,000 miles away, but before that, on Wednesday night, the comet will cross the Sun's disk and the tail will stretch out in a straight line behind it, so that if its length is sufficient, we shall pass through it.

What will happen then, or whether anything will happen that will be perceptible to the ordinary man, are questions of daily debate. Among astronomers the general opinion is that even if the tail be sufficiently long to reach us, the world generally will be unaware that it is passing through the comet's tail. . . .

## COMET MAY CAUSE AURORA

. . . The tail is composed of exceedingly tenuous gas, and the suggestion that it might contain meteors seems quite untenable, since it is only for particles whose diameter is about the same as a wave length of light—say one forty-thousandths part of an inch—that repulsive force exceeds gravitation. . . . An idea of the tenuity of the tail is given by the fact that very faint stars can be seen through the thickness of some hundreds of thousands of miles of tail, while a few feet of fog would suffice to obscure them.

Hence, there is no probability that any sensible effect will be produced on our atmosphere. . . .

ANDREW C. D. CROMMELIN
Greenwich Observatory

## CYANOGEN SEEMED TO VANISH

### Afterward Reappeared in the Tail, as Observed at Meudon

SPECIAL CABLE TO THE NEW YORK TIMES
PARIS, May 15 — My observations of Halley's Comet taken since November last have shown the presence in the tail, first, of cyanogen in the month of December, then in January, hydrocarbons, which further developed in February, March, and April, while cyanogen vanished from the spectrum. In May cyanogen again appeared.

It is not at all unreasonable to suppose that the approach of the comet to the

Sun, causing a change in the angles of the rays of light that are reflected from the atoms composing the tail, may account for the seeming disappearance of the cyanogen as well as its subsequent reappearance. Neither is the hypothesis absurd that the comet may have a perturbing influence upon the atmosphere of the Earth. This we can neither affirm nor deny.

As to contact of the comet's tail with the Earth or its atmosphere having any disastrous effect, there is nothing in astronomical history or in the present indications to justify such a fear. The gases composing the tail of the comet are exceedingly thin. I feel no apprehensions from this cause either for the Earth or for its inhabitants.

HENRY DESLANDRES
Director of the Observatory at Meudon

**MAY 17, 1910**
**PAGE 1**

### DUE IN COMET'S TAIL
### TO-MORROW, 10:50 P.M.

*It's Now 24,000,000 Miles Long,*
*and Where We'll Cross It, 150,000 to*
*1,000,000 Miles Wide*

### 1 TO 7 HOURS IN TRANSIT

*Smaller Figure Harvard's; Larger,*
*Lick Observatory's—We Ought to*
*Know the Worst by Midnight*

SPECIAL TO THE NEW YORK TIMES
CAMBRIDGE, Mass., May 16 — Prof. Edward C. Pickering of the Harvard Observatory said to-night:

"The exact time that the Earth will commence its transition through the tail of Halley's Comet next Wednesday will be 10:50 P.M. At 11:48 P.M. the transition will have been concluded.

"We do not look for any startling phenomena, but have taken every precaution to have instruments placed on Observatory Hill to record any possible effect the transition will cause, even to change of light." . . .

### COMET SCARE IN A CAR

*Passengers Thought a Wreck Was Due*
*to the Celestial Visitor*

Passengers in a crowded north-bound Eighth Avenue car to the last man and woman were convinced that the tail of Halley's Comet had side-wiped the Earth last night when as the car was passing through Columbus Circle the roof broke through with a crash and every pane of glass was shattered.

But it was not the comet that caused the trouble. Employes of a motor car company were testing a new cooling fan for automobiles when one of the blades of the fan got loose, flew through an open window on the fifth floor, and went hurtling into the roof of the car. The blade weighed about twenty pounds. One thousand revolutions a minute was the speed of the propeller-like device when it broke off. It was estimated that the piece of metal went upward at least 600 feet before the law of gravitation overcame the thrust of momentum and the blade started downward.

"It's the comet," exclaimed a woman passenger as the blade struck and splintered the roof of the car. The same idea seemed to possess every other passenger, and there was a rush for the doors. Fortunately the large hub end of the blade stuck in the roof. . . . Although the shattered glass flew in all directions, no one was hurt. . . .

Patrolman John Maine of the traffic squad caught a glimpse of the fan blade as it fell and began to scan the sky for the aeroplane from which he thought it had fallen. . . .

The aeroplane theory was accepted in all earnestness until James Murray, an employe of the motor company, went to the [police] station and put in a claim for the fan.

PARIS, May 16 — Comet suppers will be in vogue on Wednesday night at all the big cafés and restaurants.

### TOPICS OF THE TIMES

#### *Anxieties with No Basis*

While it is true that what even the most learned of astronomers know about comets is probably less than what they have still to discover it is also true that they know enough to warrant their confident assurances that nobody need worry over the happenings of to-morrow night. . . . The old ideas about the comet's closeness to human affairs lingers only as a recognized superstition, but the beliefs of innumerable centuries do not altogether disappear the moment their baselessness is revealed. Feeling survives knowing, and—well, there's no denying that a comet is an impressive spectacle.

## MAY 18, 1910
## LEAD STORY, PAGE 1

### SIX HOURS TO-NIGHT
### IN THE COMET'S TAIL

*Few New Yorkers Likely to Know
It by Ocular Demonstration,
for It May Be Cloudy*

### FOUR MILLION-MILE JOURNEY

*Takes Us Through 48 Trillion Cubic
Miles of the Tail, Weighing All
Told Half an Ounce*

BY TELEGRAPH TO THE EDITOR OF THE NEW YORK TIMES

LICK OBSERVATORY, Cal., May 17 — At least 105 degrees of the tail of Halley's Comet was visible to the naked eye this morning, corresponding in length to a space of 20,000,000 miles. The tail is probably shortening as the comet recedes from the Sun. The diameter of the tail at the point through which the earth will pass on Wednesday evening was this morning still 1,000,000 miles.

W. W. CAMPBELL
Director Lick Observatory

For six hours beginning at 10:50 o'clock tonight, New York time, according to the best calculations, this earth will pass through the tail of Halley's Comet but whether there will be much or any ocular demonstration of the fact to the ordinary man not well versed in astronomy is very much in doubt. . . .

### CHICAGO IS TERRIFIED

*Women Are Stopping Up Doors and
Windows to Keep Out Cyanogen*

SPECIAL TO THE NEW YORK TIMES

CHICAGO, May 17—Terror occasioned by the near approach of Halley's Comet has seized hold of a large part of the population of Chicago. Especially has the feminine portion succumbed. All else is forgotten. Comets and their ways and habits have been the principal topic discussed in the streets, cars, and elevated trains to-day. . . .

The principal fear is not that the comet will strike the Earth, but that the gas which it is supposed makes up the tail will wipe out all life.

"I have stopped [up] all the windows and doors in my flat to keep the gas out," said one woman over the telephone. "All the other women in the building think it is a good thing, and all are doing the same." . . . Physicians say that there were scores of calls to-day for their services from women who were suffering from hysteria. . . .

## MAY 19, 1910
## LEAD STORY, PAGE 1

### COMET GAZERS
### SEE FLASHES

*And Then at 2:30 A.M. the*
*Comet's Tail, 100 Degrees*
*Long, 10 Degrees Wide*

### EARLIER LIGHTS AURORAL

*Seen in the Northeastern Sky by*
*Miss Proctor and Other Visitors to the Times Tower*

### FIRST CONTACT UNSEEN

*Results Negative at Yerkes Observatory—Aurora*
*Lights Due to Sun Spots*

### WATCHERS AT ALL HOTELS

*Throngs Gather on the Roofs in the*
*Hope of Seeing Phenomena—East Side Excited*

Speeding by the Earth at a rate which would have carried it from this city to Chicago in about thirty seconds and across the continent in just six seconds over a minute, Halley's Comet brushed the earth with its long spreading tail last night, and few of the thousands of sky gazers who thronged Broadway, the hotel roofs, The Times tower, the river bridges, Riverside Drive, and the ferry boats were any the wiser. The Earth is supposed to have entered the tail at a point of 15,000,000 miles from the comet's head at 10:50 P.M. and to have finished the transit of a million miles about 5 o'clock this morning. The tail and the Earth passed each other at a joint speed of forty-three miles a second.

### Glimpse of the Tail at 2:30 This Morning

Between 10:50 and 11:30 P.M. Miss Mary Proctor, the astronomer, and the other watchers on top of The Times tower saw what appeared to be auroral flashes in the Northeastern sky. Miss Proctor remained on watch all night, and at 2:30 this morning, just after the moon had set, discovered a band of light 100 degrees in length stretching from the horizon at the point of sunrise and up through the great square of Pegasus and Aquarius to Aquila.

At its widest part, just beneath the first magnitude star, Altair, the width of the band was about ten degrees, and throughout its length it had a brilliance equal to that of the Milky Way, near which it terminated. The path of this band of light was very nearly that along which the comet was last seen and Miss Proctor was convinced that it was the outer boundary of the tail through which the Earth was passing. The band of light was still there at 3 o'clock this morning.

Other watchers who have seen the comet and its tail repeatedly during the last two weeks, confirmed Miss Proctor's view.

### Unseen by Prof. Jacoby

Prof. Harold Jacoby, Rutherfurd Professor of Astronomy of Columbia University, stood out on Riverside Drive from 10:30 o'clock until midnight watching for phenomena. At midnight he concluded there would be none, and remarked:

"The fact that the comet's tail has not been visible at the time of its contact with the Earth, which must now be chiefly past, is a vindication for the general belief of astronomers that the tail is so thin that its presence near us is undetectable. The wonder of the comet then becomes why so thin and sinuous a body as the tail can be seen so brightly when off in distant space." . . .

At 10 o'clock a hurry call from Larchmont arrived over the telephone at Prof. Jacoby's residence, notifying him that peculiar auroral flashes were visible along the eastern horizon.

"Yes," he remarked, "that's exactly where the offshore lighthouses cast their glimmer out to sea. . . ."

The crowd that was dense along the bridges and Riverside Drive at 10 o'clock began to dwindle at 11, and was pretty well in doors by midnight. With café and hotel parties, however, it was different. . . .

In the vicinity of Grant's Tomb most of the benches were occupied. . . . The lower east side was probably the liveliest section. . . . All along Grand Street, especially, there was a throng of excitable foreigners chatting about the comet in their native tongues and gazing at the sky. . . .

Late in the evening, some small boys climbed to the roof of 401 Grand Street and sent up a toy balloon with a red light attached. It shot skyward and began drifting eastward. . . . On the Williamsburg Bridge some 20,000 people had gathered to watch for whatever phenomena there might be. The bridge crowd soon caught sight of the balloon, and across the bridge ran the shout:

"There is the comet, look!" They were still looking when the toy balloon passed out of sight. . . .

At about 8:30 o'clock there was a demonstration in front of Old St. Patrick's Cathedral in Mott Street near Prince. A long procession of Italian children, clad in white, filed past the church chanting the Litany of the Blessed Virgin. . . .

While several hundred men and women were gazing at the sky from the roof of the Waldorf-Astoria, a flashlight was set off unawares by a photographer. The brilliant flash of light and the noise made by the explosion caused the watchers to think that the crack of doom had really arrived, and there was much excitement for a few moments. Several women screamed but their fears were quickly appeased. . . . A huge telescope was operated in the centre of the roof, and there the watchers stood in line to get a peep at anything the starry firmament had to offer. . . .

The throng was considerably increased when 200 members of the National Association of Manufacturers, with their wives, came up after their dinner. "Uncle Joe" Cannon [Speaker of the House of Representatives, Joseph Cannon], with a big black cigar between his lips, seemed to enjoy the scene. . . .

YERKES OBSERVATORY, WILLIAMS BAY, Wis., Thursday, May 19 — "We have passed through the comet's tail and we are no wiser than we were before."

Prof. Frost, head of Yerkes Observatory, thus summarized the results of the night's observations at 1 o'clock this morning. . . .

BERLIN, May 18 — Countless "comet parties" have been organized for tonight, some to Kreuzberg Hill, an eminence on the southern outskirts of this city, and others to the forest of Grunewald, lying between Berlin and Potsdam. . . .

GENEVA, May 18 — American visitors have to-day been heading a rush to the highest Alpine resorts in the funicular cars in order to view the comet. . . .

NIGHT SERVICES IN RUSSIA

ST. PETERSBURG, May 18 — Though the newspapers publish reassuring articles, the passage through the tail of Halley's Comet causes considerable fear.

Many persons have decided to pass to-night in churches, where continuous prayers have been ordered.

LONDON, Thursday, May 19 — A telegram to The Daily Mail from Johannesburg says . . . there is an extraordinary amount of nervousness. . . . The lower class foreign population and the poorer Dutch and colored people are particularly anxious and seem to anticipate some disaster.

ASHEVILLE, N.C., May 18 — The negroes of Asheville were in a state of frenzy to-night, believing that the end of the world was at hand. . . . According to police court records, crime has slumped remarkably. . . . Nor could a Negro be hired for "love or money," for they said there would be no more paydays.

WILKESBARRE, Penn., May 18 — Several thousand mine workers of the anthracite region, chiefly foreigners, refused to enter the mines.

SAN JUAN, Puerto Rico, May 18 — Hundreds of Puerto Ricans paraded in the streets . . . carrying candles and chanting prayers. . . .

## SOME DRIVEN TO SUICIDE

### *Others Become Temporarily Insane from Brooding Over Comet*

SPECIAL TO THE NEW YORK TIMES

CHICAGO, May 18 — The approach of the comet affected Chicago people in divers ways. Some it drove temporarily and harmlessly insane, and others developed suicidal mania.

Blanche Covington made up her mind that there was no escape from the comet and that it would kill everybody in Chicago. She had difficulty in convincing her friends, but this did not change her own opinion. Dreading the suffering that she might have to undergo she locked herself in a room and turned on the gas. Mrs. Marie Welch called a policeman, and with his aid Miss Covington was rescued.

Fear of the comet is believed to have driven Mrs. Sophie Houge, 90 years old, insane. She committed suicide to-day by inhaling illuminating gas.

Samuel Popowski declared that the tail of the comet was striking him all the time, and that it was beating him into shreds. City Physician Baldwin pronounced him insane.

## MAY 20, 1910
## LEAD STORY, PAGE 1

### DIDN'T GET THROUGH
### THE COMET'S TAIL

### *Observatories Confirm Times's Unexpected Discovery of It in the East Yesterday Morning*

### ALL ASK: WHERE IS IT NOW?

### *Can It Be That Band Across the Sun the Yerkes Observatory Detected Yesterday?—Varied Views*

### TIMES OBSERVATIONS CONFIRMED

[Several] dispatches from leading astronomers were received by The Times last night confirming the unexpected discovery of the comet's tail in the east when it should have been in the west, as announced in The Times yesterday morning.

SAN JOSE, Cal., May 19 — The object which you saw this morning was the brighter part of the comet's tail. Our observations agree with yours and extended the tail to the Milky Way. We have this evening observed the nucleus exactly in the predicted position. No other part of the comet certainly visible in evening sky. . . .

> W. W. CAMPBELL
> Director Lick Observatory

The Earth, apparently, did not pass through the comet's tail, as generally predicted by astronomers, between the hours of 10:50 on Wednesday night and 4:50 yesterday morning, after all. In late editions yesterday The Times was able to announce that from observations taken on the tower of The Times Building between 2:30 and 8:15 A.M. the wanderer's tail was still in the eastern sky at a time when the Earth should have been passing through it preparatory to its being seen last night in the west.

Sun spots seen Wednesday afternoon, followed by brilliant displays of northern lights last night, and these in turn succeeded by varied reports of fiery streamers shooting across the horizon to the southwest had been passed by the astronomers as having absolutely no direct connection with the comet. But the band across the Sun was another story.

"Although I cannot advance an opinion at this time," said Prof. Frost [E. B. Frost of the Yerkes Observatory], "I can see no other cause but the comet for the appearance of the spectrum." . . .

Shattering all scientific calculations and puzzling the astronomers, the tail of Halley's Comet appeared in the eastern sky early to-day at a time when the authorities had agreed it would be in the west. . . . Leading astronomers throughout the world strove yesterday to find some explanation for the trick Halley's Comet, and particularly its tail, played on them and the rest of the world Wednesday night.

One theory advanced was that the comet had actually dropped its tail, which thereupon had drifted off into space. . . .

Prof. Harold Jacoby of Columbia said he was never more surprised than when he read in The Times yesterday morning that the Earth had evidently not been through the comet's tail at all but that the tail had actually been observed till nearly daybreak by Miss Proctor from The Times tower.

Prof. Jacoby expressed his admiration for the patience and perseverance of Miss Proctor, which made possible the announcement to the Times's readers. . . .

**Miss Proctor's Account of Her Sighting Thursday Morning**
. . . At 2:30 o'clock the Moon, ruddy in hue, was low down in the western sky. Looking again in the direction of the eastern horizon, a white mist could be seen drifting over the [Queensboro] bridge, and reaching upward beneath the Square of Pegasus. A soft glow of grayish hue now became plainly visible, spreading from Pegasus as far as Cassiopeia's chair. The light of the Moon no longer interfering made this observation possible. At 2:34 o'clock this soft glow of grayish hue extended in the northeastern sky to over the left of the Queensboro Bridge, as seen by the observers in the tower . . . At 4:25 o'clock red streaks made their appearance in the eastern sky, and Venus paled as rosy-fingered dawn drew aside the curtain of day. [She speculated in the next day's edition that the comet's tail may have missed the Earth by 197,000 miles.]

## HALLEY'S COMET CLUB

About the only tangible thing the comet has left along Broadway is the Comet Club . . . [formed at the Knickerbocker Hotel to prepare for the next appearance of Halley's Comet].

# EDITORIAL

## THE COMET

Considerable additions to the public stock of knowledge about comets have resulted from the untiring scrutiny to which Halley's Comet has been subjected since it first came within the range of our vision a few weeks ago. As a sort of bull [sic] against this and all other comets, it may be remarked that these additions to our knowledge are chiefly negative. . . .

# The Magnitude Scale of Brightness

The magnitude scale is in a logarithmic mode, so that magnitude *differences* correspond to *ratios* of actual energy. Thus a difference of 5 magnitude steps indicates a ratio of exactly 100; each magnitude step is a factor of a little more than 2.5 in real energy. In other words, a star of magnitude 5 is 2.5 times brighter than one of magnitude 6. There are historic reasons why increasing magnitude numbers refer to decreasing brightnesses, but we have similar paradoxes in everyday life such as nail sizes and wire gauges.

The apparent magnitude of an object is a measure of how bright it appears to the observer. In the case of comets, the amount of energy they radiate is diluted by the effects of distance. If a comet moves twice as far away and emits the same amount of energy, it will appeaar ¼ as bright as it was first discerned, because light varies according to the inverse square of distance between its source and the observer. But the amount of energy the comet is emitting at any given time is highly dependent on its distance from the Sun and on its reaction to solar radiation.

The amount of energy the comet receives from the Sun follows the same sort of inverse square law that applies to source and observer. Here the source is the Sun and the observer is the comet. If the object we are observing happens to be an asteroid that simply reflects sunlight, we now have all we need to know—distance from Sun to body, distance from body to us—to predict the brightness behavior of the body. But the reactive nature of the comet now steps into the picture to alter its simplicity.

As the comet nears the Sun, its frozen gases sublime and expand in a huge cloud surrounding the simple, reflective nucleus. The cloud now also contains solid fragments of the nucleus, each a small mirror, so that the "screen" available to reflect sunlight is now larger than the simple nucleus. The comet now reflects (radiates) more energy than a nonreactive body in the same geometric circumstances. It is often convenient for the astronomer to try to take this reaction into account by increasing the dependence on the distance to the Sun from inverse square to inverse fourth power. In this case, a change of 2 in distance results in a ratio of 16 in brightness. Recall the ratio of 4 for the inverse square law.

If the comet contains much material that fluoresces—translates normally invisible ultraviolet sunlight into visible colors—there is a source of radiant energy in addition to those mentioned above. Astronomers attempt to account for this by using an inverse sixth power law. Now a change of 2 in solar distance results in a ratio of 256 in energy output. (Some astronomers felt justified in using this law for Comet Kohoutek in 1973—thus the inflated predictions of brightness.)

A comet does not necessarily follow one of these neat laws, but we use them for convenience of calculation in estimating brightness behavior. (Kohoutek followed a law whose power was a little *less* than inverse fourth!)

Observations of the brightness of a comet are used with the power laws and adjusted for the laws' effects in order to determine an "absolute magnitude," or the magnitude it would appear to have if it were one astronomical unit from both the Sun and the Earth. Astronomers ultimately use all observations of brightness and distances to determine variations in the absolute magnitude and the actual "power" the beast is using.

$$m = H + Nx2.5 \log r + 2 \times 2.5 \log (\text{"delta"}).$$

**m** is observed apparent magnitude, various subscripts referring to total, nuclear, etc.

**H** is the absolute magnitude.

**N** is the power: 2 for inverse square, 4, 6, etc.

**r** is Sun-comet distance.

**"delta"** is Earth-comet distance.

# Aids to Observing the Comet

## Associations

Amateurs looking for guidance can find it through any number of associations in the United States and around the world. Membership in these groups often includes a subscription to their periodicals.

The Amateur Observers Society of New York City, 18 Hastings Drive, North Merrick, New York 11566. (Telephone number not available.) Samuel Storch, director.

The American Association of Variable Star Observers (AAVSO), 187 Concord Avenue, Cambridge, Massachusetts 02138. (Telephone number not available.) Janet Mattei, director. Since 1911 this group has encouraged the systematic observation of variable stars.

The Association of Lunar and Planetary Observers, P.O. Box 3AZ, University Park, New Mexico 88003. (Telephone number not available.) A section of the association is devoted to comets.

The Astronomical League, P.O. Box 12821, Tucson, Arizona 85732. Don Archer, executive secretary, (602) 790-8471; David Levy, assistant, (602) 762-5638. This is the umbrella group for 160 amateur clubs throughout the United States.

The Astronomical Society of the Pacific, 1290 24th Avenue, San Francisco, California 94122. (Telephone number not available.) Andrew Fraknoi, director. Among its functions, the society publishes *Mercury* magazine.

The Harvard-Smithsonian Center for Astrophysics. 60 Garden Street, Cambridge, Massachusetts 02138. (617) 495-7461. Irwin Shapiro, director. Jim Cornell, public relations. This includes both Harvard and the Smithsonian Institution.

International Halley's Watch (IHW), Pasadena, California. (818) 793-5100. The IHW's main compendium of information is the *Amateur Observer's Bulletin*, Planetary Society, P.O. Box 91687, 110 South Euclid, Pasadena, California 91109. Stephen Edberg, editor.

The Royal Astronomical Society of Canada, 136 Dupont Street, Toronto, Ontario M5RIV2. (416) 924-7973. This group has clubs from eastern to western Canada.

The Western Amateur Astronomers, P.O. Box 2316, Palm Desert, California 92261. (619) 346-2524. Ashley McDermott, secretary.

## *Books*

A great many books on astronomy in general and comets in particular should prove useful for the return of Halley's Comet. Here are some of them.

*All About Telescopes* by Sam Brown (Publication E9094 or E9385, U.S.A. 1981.) Edmund Scientific Company, 101 East Gloucester Pike, Barrington, N.J. 08007.

*The Amateur Astronomer's Handbook* by James Muirden. New York: Harper & Row, 1983.
Basic information aimed toward helping the reader become an accomplished observer, from what to look for when selecting equipment to detailed techniques of observation.

*Astronomy: The Cosmic Journey* by William K. Hartman. Belmont, Calif.: Wadsworth Publishing, 1978.
Some reviews called it the finest introductory college text on astronomy available. Good for parents and teachers as well.

*Astronomy with Binoculars* by James Muirden. New York: Crowell, 1979.
Explains how to select binoculars and use them to observe planets and other astronomical objects, including comets, meteors, and novas.

*Binoculars and All-Purpose Telescopes* by Henry E. Paul. New York: Amphoto, 1964.
A handbook for prospective purchasers.

*Burnham's Celestial Handbook* by Robert Burnham, Jr. New York: Dover, 1978.
A major reference work for deep-sky observing, arranged alphabetically by constellation.

*Comets: Vagabonds of Space* by David A. Seargent. Garden City, N.Y.: Doubleday, 1982.

This book discusses the physical and orbital characteristics of comets, the ways they are discovered, and their possible origins, with descriptions of some of the more spectacular and famous comets.

*Comets Booklet* is a free booklet by the staff of the Smithsonian Institution that can be obtained by writing to the Smithsonian Astrophysical Observatory, 60 Garden Street, Cambridge, Massachusetts 02138.

*Comet Halley's Handbook* is published by Caltech in Pasadena and written by Donald K. Yeomans.

*The Comet Is Coming* by Nigel Calder. New York: Penguin, 1982.

The history of comets as well as the theories. It includes specific information on Halley's Comet.

*A Complete Manual of Amateur Astronomy* by P. Clay Sherrod. Englewood Cliffs, N.J.: Prentice-Hall Inc., 1981.

Includes tips on dozens of research projects suitable for amateur astronomers with modest equipment, plus much practical observing data.

*A Field Guide to the Stars and Planets* by Donald H. Menzel and Jay M. Pasachoff. Peterson Field Guide Service, 2nd ed. (revised). Boston: Houghton Mifflin, 1983.

A pocket guide to the nighttime sky. Included are 72 monthly sky maps, 52 detailed charts of the entire sky showing 25,000 stars to magnitude 7.5, plus over 230 photographs.

*Guideposts to the Stars* by Leslie C. Peltier. New York: Macmillan, 1972.

Peltier's second book is aimed at advanced elementary and early secondary schoolchildren; it concentrates on the stars and the constellations.

*The Milky Way* by Priscilla J. and Bart J. Bok. 5th ed. Cambridge, Mass.: Harvard, 1981.

A guide to our galaxy by two articulate astronomers.

*Norton's Star Atlas* by Arthur P. Norton and Inglis J. Gall. 16th ed. Edited by Gilbert Southerswaite. Cambridge, Mass.: Sky Publishing, 1910, 1978.

One of the best portable star atlases around. This atlas also contains a lunar map with 326 features.

*Observational Astronomy for Amateurs* by J. B. Sidgwick. New York: Dover, 1981.

The book describes observational techniques needed by advanced amateurs in various fields. Each chapter is devoted to a single planet or phenomenon.

*The Observer's Handbook* is published by The Royal Astronomical Society of Canada in Toronto. It is an annual guide to positions of the planets, to times for eclipses, and to what special events can be seen from night to night.

*Planets of Rock and Ice: From Mercury to the Moons of Saturn* by Clark R. Chapman. New York: Scribner's, 1982.
A summary of what is known about the planets.

*Starlight Nights: The Adventures of a Star Gazer* by Leslie C. Peltier. Cambridge, Mass.: Sky Publishing, 1980.
A man who has been observing the night sky for over sixty years tells his story.

*Stars: A Golden Guide* by Herbert S. Zim and Robert H. Baker. New York: Western Publishing Co., 1975.
Profusely illustrated, and compact.

*The Stars Belong to Everyone* by Helen Sawyer Hogg. Garden City, N.Y.: Doubleday, 1976.
An introduction to astronomy.

*The Telescope* by Louis Bell. New York: Dover.
First published in 1922, this remains a classic reference.

*The Telescope Handbook and Star Atlas* by Neale E. Howard. 2nd ed. New York: Crowell, 1975.
Clear diagrams; contains a star atlas.

*Telescopes for Skygazing* by Henry E. Paul. 3rd ed. Garden City, N.Y.: Amphoto, 1976.
Considered a bible of telescope owners and enthusiasts. Copies can be obtained from Sky Publishing Corporation, 49 Bay State Road, Cambridge, Massachusetts 02138.

## *Manufacturers of Optics*

Inclusion in this list is not intended to suggest endorsement.

Bushnell Optical, 2828 East Foothill Boulevard, Pasadena, California 91107. (818) 577-1500.

Celestron International, Columbia Street, Torrance, California 90503. (213) 328-9560. A recently introduced telescope is the Comet Catcher.

Edmund Scientific Company, 101 East Gloucester Pike, Barrington, New Jersey 08007. (609) 547-3488. This company manufactures the very popular 4-inch Astroscan, which provides a relatively wide field of view.

Image Point Company, 831 North Swan, Tucson, Arizona 85711. (602) 327-6643.

Lumicon, 2111 Research Drive 5, Livermore, California 94550. (415) 447-9570.

Meade Instruments Corporation, 1675 Toronto Way, Costa Mesa, California 92676. (Telephone number not available.)

Orion Telescopes, P.O. Box 1158-T, Santa Cruz, California 95061. (408) 476-8715.

Questar Corporation, P.O. Box C, New Hope, Pennsylvania 18938. (215) 862-2000.

Star-Liner Company, 1106 South Columbus Boulevard, Tucson, Arizona 85711. (602) 795-3361.

Tasco Sales, 7600 N.W. 26th Street, Miami, Florida 33122. (305) 591-3670.

Unitron Instruments, 175 Express Street, Plainview, New York 11803. (516) 822-4601.

## PERIODICALS

The publications listed below range from elementary to technical and single topic to broad spectrum. Write to the addresses listed for current subscription charges.

*AAS Photo Bulletin*, Robert J. Leacock, Subscription Manager, 211 Space Sciences Building, University of Florida, Gainesville, Florida 32611.

*Astronomy*, Astromedia Corp., 625 E. St. Paul Ave., P.O. Box 92788, Milwaukee, Wisconsin 53202.

*Comet News Service*, P.O. Box TDR No. 92, Truckee, California 95734.

*Griffith Observer*, Griffith Observatory, 2800 East Observatory Road, Los Angeles, California 90027.

*Halley's Comet Watch Newsletter*, 1 Smith Court, Box 188, Vincentown, New Jersey 08098.

*International Astronomical Union Circulars and IAU Telegrams*, Central Bureau for Astronomical Telegrams, Smithsonian Astrophysical Observatory, 60 Garden St., Cambridge, Massachusetts 02138.

*International Comet Quarterly*, Smithsonian Astrophysical Observatory, 60 Garden St., Cambridge, Massachusetts 02138. Daniel Green, editor.

*International Halley Watch Amateur Observer's Bulletin*, Planetary Society, P.O. Box 91687, Pasadena, California 91109.

*Journal of the ALPO/The Strolling Astronomer*, Association of Lunar and Planetary Observers, P.O. Box 3AZ, University Park, New Mexico 88003.

*Mercury*, Astronomical Society of the Pacific, 1290 24th Avenue, San Francisco, California 94122.

*Meteor News*, c/o Wanda Simmons, Route 3, Box 424-99, Callahan, Florida 32011.

*The Minor Planet Bulletin*, Derald D. Nye, Route 7, Box 511, Tucson, Arizona 85747.

*Odyssey*, Astromedia Corporation, 625 E. St. Paul Ave., P.O. Box 92788, Milwaukee, Wisconsin 53202. (A children's-level publication.)

*Sky and Telescope*, Sky Publishing Corporation, 49 Bay State Road, Cambridge, Massachusetts 02138.

*Sky Calendar*, Abrams Planetarium, Michigan State University, East Lansing, Michigan 48824–1324.

*Tonight's Asteroids*, Dr. J. U. Gunter, 1411 North Mangum St., Durham, North Carolina 27701. (Enclose a self-addressed, stamped envelope for reply.)

# Index